Encounters of Evangelisation

making the most of opportunities through the parish

Diana Klein

Published by Redemptorist Publications
Alphonsus House, Chawton, Hampshire, GU34 3HQ, UK
Tel: +44 (0) 420 88222 Fax: +44 (0) 420 88805

E-mail: rp@rpbooks.co.uk web: www.rpbooks.co.uk

copyright © Redemptorist Publications 2017

First published August 2017

Editor: Bahram Francis Rafat

ISBN: 978-0-85231-488-3

All rights reserved. No part of this publication may be reproduced, stored in a retrieval system, or transmitted in any form or by any means, electronic, mechanical, photocopying, recording or otherwise, without prior permission from Redemptorist Publications.

A moral right of the authors to be identified as the authors of this work has been asserted in accordance with the Copyright, Designs and Patents Act 1988.

A CIP catalogue record for this book is available from the British Library.

The publisher gratefully acknowledges permission to use the following copyright materials:

We are grateful to Thomas Groome for allowing us to use an excerpt from his book *Christian Religious Education – Sharing Our Story and Vision* (New York: Harper Collins Publishers, 1980).

We are very grateful to *The Tablet* (www.thetablet.co.uk) for granting us permission to use ideas and excerpts from the Parish Practice page and *The Pastoral Review* (www.thepastoralreview.org) for granting us permission to use ideas and excerpts from articles; we are also grateful to the authors of the original articles. Contributors include: Fr Bernard Cotter, Kasia Greenwood, Fr Tom Grufferty, Sheila Keefe, Jane Shields, Fr Ulick Loring and Liz O'Brien.

Excerpts from the *New Revised Standard Version of the Bible: Anglicised Edition*, © 1989, 1995, Division of Christian Education of the National Council of the Churches of Christ in the United States of America. Used by permission. All rights reserved.

Vatican documents are quoted from the Vatican website (www.vatican.va).

Picture credits

p.7 official picture of Bishop Nicholas Hudson © Mazur/Diocese of Westminster; p.10, p.11 the ambo/lectern in Sacred Heart and Mary Immaculate, Mill Hill, London © Kim Llewellyn; p.20 *Road to Emmaus* by Duccio di Buoninsegna: in the public domain; p.23 *Supper at Emmaus* by Caravaggio (c. 1600-01): in the public domain; p.25 Two boys on the road to Mua © Diana Klein 1994; p.31 Photo of Archbishop Longley © St Vincent de Paul Redditch Conference; p.42 © John McCorkell 2016 (John McCorkell, Diversity Day) (www.itsallnormal.com); p.51 Lily Kline, CICCA © Diana Klein 2009; p.54 Ant and Karen's wedding, © Diana Klein 2010; p.75 Pope hearing confession © Reuters; p.91 Vincent de Paul sitting among the poor as one of them, centrepiece of a triptych by Kurt Weither from Sacred Heart and Mary Immaculate, Mill Hill, London, photo © Diana Klein; p.95 Small Christian Community in Malawi © Diana Klein 2006.

Printed by Portland Print, Kettering, NN16 8UN

This book is dedicated to

Rev. Dr Robert Kaggwa MAfr PhD (1959-2015)

and to the many other Missionaries of Africa (White Fathers),

Vincentians and others

who have taught me about evangelisation

BIOGRAPHY

Diana Klein is editor of the Parish Practice and Schools Practice Pages of *The Tablet*. She worked for Westminster Diocese for sixteen years as a catechist and as Catechetical Adviser with their Agency for Evangelisation before retiring in 2011. She studied at the Missionary Institute London and has a Batchelor's Degree in Theology for Ministry and a Master's Degree in Applied Theology (Mission Studies). She was a Visiting Lecturer at the MIL, at Campion House and at Heythrop College. She has written many articles for *The Tablet, The Pastoral Review* and other publications on the subject of evangelisation through the brief and personal encounters people have in pastoral work and catechesis. Her work includes the following:

How to Survive Working in a Catholic Parish, which she co-authored with Bernard Cotter (published in 2016 by Redemptorist Publications)

Symbols of Faith – faith formation and sacramental preparation for people with learning disabilities (published in 2014 by Redemptorist Publications)

The Christ we Proclaim – Christian initiation for children of catechetical age (*CICCA*) (published in 2010 online by Westminster Diocese)

Preparing to be Confirmed (published in 2002 by McCrimmons Publications)

CONTENTS

FOREWORD by Bishop Nicholas Hudson 7

INTRODUCTION 8

CHAPTER ONE
Where are you, God? 13

CHAPTER TWO
The disciples encounter Jesus 21

CHAPTER THREE
Most of Jesus' ministry took place out in
the open 27

CHAPTER FOUR
About welcoming 35

CHAPTER FIVE
Brief encounters through baptisms, weddings
and funerals 45

CHAPTER SIX
Brief encounters of evangelisation in our parish
catechetical programmes 61

CHAPTER SEVEN
Reaching out to non-churchgoing Catholics 79

CHAPTER EIGHT
Reaching out to those who are sick and poor 85

CHAPTER NINE
When two or three are gathered in my name,
I am there 93

CHAPTER TEN
Go tell everyone the news that the kingdom
of God has come 99

REFERENCES AND RESOURCES 101

FOREWORD

"Jesus wants us to touch the suffering flesh of others… Whenever we do so, our lives become wonderfully complicated and we experience intensely what it is to be a people, to be part of a people." This is the core message of Pope Francis when he describes "the joy of the Gospel" (*Evangelii Gaudium,* 271). It is the core message of Diana Klein's *Encounters of Evangelisation*.

Successive Popes have called the Church to a New Evangelisation. The New Evangelisation calls every member of the Church to be a missionary disciple. Diana Klein speaks with the voice of one such missionary disciple. She writes out of a conviction that it is through relationship that we communicate Christ. She recounts a host of encounters which speak of meeting Christ in others.

Encounters of Evangelisation is shot through with the joy of encounter. Like Cleopas and the other disciple who met Him on the road to Emmaus, the author knows from experience the value of recalling, recounting and reflecting on encounter with the Risen One. She weaves into the testimony of countless others the telling of her own story – in a way which will encourage the reader to reflect on their own.

I welcome *Encounters of Evangelisation* as a tool to be harnessed to the New Evangelisation. Whether we be catechists, teachers, preachers or individuals seeking simply to deepen our relationship with Christ, *Encounters of Evangelisation* will urge and challenge us to make our parishes, our schools, our homes – and indeed our hearts – places of profound welcome.

I pray the Lord will be close to you in your reading of this book and that it will lead you indeed to encounter the Lord Jesus in ways new and surprising.

Yours devotedly in Christ

✠ Nicholas Hudson
Auxiliary Bishop of Westminster

INTRODUCTION

Although fewer people say they think the Church is relevant today, people still turn to the Church at key moments in their lives. We cannot ignore the opportunities available to us in the often brief encounters of evangelisation these key moments offer us.

I recall one such key moment that took place after the bombings of 7/7 in 2005. A young Nigerian parishioner in Mill Hill, Anthony Fatayi-Williams, was killed in the bus bomb on his way to his job in the City. Naturally, the parish was united in praying for him and his family, but we asked what more we could do to support the family in these tragic circumstances. They asked for an evening of prayer following Mass with adoration of the Blessed Sacrament. The choir and musicians came to help and the church was filled with family, friends, neighbours, parishioners and colleagues from the City – Christian, Muslim, Jewish, Sikh and Hindu.

We placed fifty-four candles on a table at the back of the church – one for each person known to have died in the blasts. While the Blessed Sacrament was exposed, people were invited to light one of the candles and bring it forward and place it on the candle stands at the front of the church. After the candles were all brought forward, more people went to the back of the church and asked for candles. The people kept coming; more and more joined the procession until the candle stands were full and they overflowed on to the sanctuary floor. There were hundreds of them. The liturgy seemed to take on a life of its own. This moving procession touched all of us who were there – those of our faith, those of other faiths and those of none.

During the procession, we sang the hymn "My God Loves Me" in the background. This simple action conveyed powerfully our belief in God's love for us which, of course, is what we are supposed to do. It was a moment when I could feel Christ really present with us as we gathered, sympathising with us and caring for us and telling us that he, too, had died; but he rose from the dead. Somehow, this gave meaning to Anthony's death and it gave us hope in this time of sorrow. For many, it was a brief encounter with Christ; it was a moment of evangelisation. As the Home Mission Desk of the Bishops' Conference of England and Wales reminds us, "Evangelisation is the sharing of the Good News of Jesus and the starting point is our relationship with him. It's about proclaiming our faith in him, by living it out in service and witness."

Introduction

The mission of the Church, and therefore of every Christian, is to continue the work of evangelisation initiated by Christ. This book will explore the moments of evangelisation we have with people as we journey through life in our families, in our parishes, at our places of work – in all the places we meet people who are searching for faith or for meaning in their lives. This book shares real experiences of people who are actively involved in evangelisation. It is not a heavy-duty textbook, but reflective, inviting material that challenges us gently to review our approach to sharing the Good News and highlights encounters that we can easily miss or overlook.

We meet couples who want to get married or parents who want their baby baptised, and, although they don't come to church, they want God to bless them and they don't know how to go about asking for that blessing. We find ourselves in conversations with Catholics who will regularly be coming to Mass – but they have never been evangelised – and our encounter with them may be the invitation they need to go another mile on their faith journey. And we meet people who are asking for answers to the "big" questions we all ask. Some of them may be looking for support because they are having a crisis in their marriage or because someone close to them has been diagnosed with a terminal illness or has just died. All these meetings can be called key moments.

The sociological changes that have taken place in recent decades demand a transformation in the way we, the Church, encounter people today. Many of the structures and props we have relied on have disappeared or are disappearing and we need new methods and approaches. Almost without noticing it, we have begun to move from being a Church which is locked up and inward-looking to being a *pilgrim* Church which looks outwards with courage, confidence and hope. And we need all these virtues, as well as humility. The world is not always welcoming but we need to welcome all, for Christ is the key to happiness and we are pilgrims on our journey to him, and we should do our best to invite everyone to him, to his Father's house.

> *"Evangelisation is the sharing of the Good News of Jesus and the starting point is our relationship with him. It's about proclaiming our faith in him, by living it out in service and witness"*

We need to become new evangelisers. We are learning that what wins people over is the way we love one another when we are hurting and messy. It is the way we welcome them with a smile in a non-judgemental way with love and with hope. It's the way we treat one another and talk about one another. And, it's about being willing to share our testimony – a powerful way to evangelise – with or without words.

This book includes theory and practice. It begins with an introductory chapter giving a short history of how our understanding of evangelisation has been developing in recent years and how evangelisation happens in the context in which we find ourselves. If we are true to a real dynamic in the understanding of Christianity today, culture and history must be *unpacked* to help people in the task of evangelisation. The main body of the book will comprise stories of the various times and ways in which we encounter Christ through others or others encounter Christ in us. My hope is that the stories will spark memories of the times when we have made a conscious choice to know and follow Jesus and that these memories will reaffirm our desire to draw others to Christ.

This book is not just for those actively involved in ministry – and it's not just for those who do not know Christ. Many Catholics of our day know a certain amount about him from the teaching of the Church, but they lack direct personal familiarity. When Pope St John Paul II spoke of the "new evangelisation" he was talking about the need to re-evangelise those traditionally Christian countries that have been weakened by a process of secularisation.

The picture opposite is of the lectern in the Catholic parish church of the Sacred Heart and Mary Immaculate, Mill Hill. The inscription is *evangelizare pauperibus misit me,* "he sent me to bring good news to the poor". It has a special significance for me. The lectern is where the Gospel is read, the Good News of Jesus Christ. I reflected on the words on the lectern many times, especially how Jesus sends "me".

I hope this book will help inspire people in their awareness of their own continuing need to be evangelised and in their desire to be evangelisers of others.

CHAPTER ONE

WHERE ARE YOU, GOD?

Be prepared to give an answer

"Always be prepared to give an answer to everyone who asks you to give the reason for the hope that you have and do this with gentleness and respect" (1 Peter 3:15).

Many of us have asked where God is when we don't know what to do; we ask where God is in a crisis or when we need him. We all have stories of how God has drawn us to himself and how he makes himself present to us. Evangelisation is about preaching the Gospel message (the kerygma) and it is also about sharing our personal experiences of how Jesus is active and involved in our lives. It's about why we believe and how we came to know God's saving love.

Finding the right words or knowing which part of your life to share is not always easy. One way to do this is to spend time reflecting and remembering the goodness of God in our lives. As Pope Francis has said, "The joy of evangelising always arises from grateful remembrance: it is a grace we constantly need to implore... The believer is essentially one who remembers" (*Evangelii Gaudium,* "The Joy of the Gospel", 13).

Memories

The words "I love you" are good to hear. We all enjoy remembering when we have heard them said to us. This is because the one thing we all have in common is our need to love and to be loved – especially by the ones we love. The context in which the words affirming love are said matters. For example, a new parent will tell their baby that they love her or him. At different times in the lives of a couple, they may say "I love you" to each other. The words are the same – whether they are those spoken in that moment of first love or as a newly married couple, whether they are said during an unsettling period of a mid-life crisis or a contented old age.

When we remember these experiences in our lives, we relive the experience; and, if we share those memories with others, we are inviting them to enter into the experience themselves – and it can become alive for them too. Authentic conversation means understanding things in new ways; it means being open to new possibilities because, when we really listen to the memories of another, we do not come away unchanged.

We share not only our personal memories; we share the wider memories of our society. Things that happened long ago are still experienced as real and are shared with others. For example, as a member of the Jewish people, Jesus shared a memory focused on God's liberation of his people from slavery in Egypt. Each year, the words and gestures of the Passover meal keep the memory of God's works alive. It is not a repetition of an ancient ritual; through the celebration, the participants become intensely aware that they are experiencing God's freedom in the present moment. They recognise the hope and joy of God's desire to bring the same freedom to their lives – and they recall God's actions of the past, celebrate his present activity and look to the future with hope.

It was in the context of the Passover that Jesus instituted the Eucharist. And, when we gather to share the story of Jesus' life, death and resurrection, we too do much more than recall a series of past events. In the present moment, we experience here and now his saving presence among us and we too look forward with hope to the future.

Evangelisation is the basic commitment of the Church

In the Introduction, we said that evangelisation is the sharing of the Good News of Jesus and the starting point is our relationship with him. It's about proclaiming our faith in him, by living it out in service and witness. The idea underlying it is that the Christian faith has to be shared by means of an active apostolate. The spreading and deepening of the Christian faith depends upon such faith-sharing. People are converted to Christ by hearing the Good News of Jesus Christ from an evangeliser.

> *"It was in the context of the Passover that Jesus instituted the Eucharist"*

The word evangelisation comes from the Greek term *euangelion*, meaning "good news"; it's about bringing the Good News "to the oppressed, to bind up the broken hearted, to proclaim liberty to the captives and release to the prisoners" (Isaiah 61:1). Isaiah foreshadows the Good News. Jesus preached God's kingdom; he spent his public life among the sick, the afflicted and the outcasts.

The Christian Gospel is therefore the Good News of Jesus Christ, the fulfilment of the promised kingdom. To evangelise is to make known the Good News of Jesus Christ and it is about sharing our personal experience of it.

Evangelisation must be contextual

Biblical study has come to recognise the importance of studying the biblical text both in the context of the text itself and in the context of present-day audiences. Contextualisation takes into account the spirit and message of the Gospel together with the tradition of the people, the culture in which we are evangelising and social change in that culture.

We read in John's Gospel, "and the Word became flesh and lived among us" (John 1:14). If the Word has become flesh, he has not ceased to be God. This is given expression here in the Greek verb *skenoun* – better translated, perhaps, as "making a dwelling", or "pitching a tent" and it has important Old Testament associations. The theme of tenting is found in Exodus (25:8-9) where Israel is told to make a tent (a tabernacle – *skene*) so that God can dwell among his people.

The people of Israel longed to be in the presence of God. Provided God was dwelling among them they felt safe. They saw the Temple as the visible sign of God's presence. Indeed, to enter the Temple was to enter the very presence of God – to savour the sweetness of the Lord. As long as they could see the Temple standing strong and secure in their midst they felt safe. In the fullness of time, God came to dwell among us in the person of Jesus, the new Temple of God. Then Jesus called his followers, like Peter and Andrew, James and John, to take his presence to others. The core of his message, then as now, was amazingly simple. God is very close to us. He is indeed, within us. He is in everybody who touches our lives. Humanity's encounter with the divine in Christ was (and is) contextual.

This quote from John's Gospel shows how important it is to understand the context of scripture – or we might miss an important principle. In this case, I wonder if the bland translation of the word *skenoun* in this passage as "lived" instead of "tented" or "tabernacled" has not sufficiently communicated the core of Jesus' message that God is so close to us that he is within us and he wants us to take his presence to others.

Contextualisation

The word "contextualisation" started coming to the Church's attention in the 1950s in parts of Africa and Asia – where there was a growing sense that the theologies inherited from the older churches of Europe and the North American community had been marred by both a lack of awareness of, and a lack of respect for, the grace of God to be found in the values of non-European cultures and religions and they did not fit well into the quite different cultural circumstances in Africa and Asia.

There were widespread feelings of dissatisfaction with classical approaches to theology and the oppressive nature of older approaches to theologies in Europe and in North America too. Social and political circumstances in the twentieth century (and particularly in the time leading up to Vatican II) criticised the oppressive nature of approaches which were filled with assumptions of male superiority and which produced distortions regarding the notion of God, liturgical language and the role of women in ministry – among other things.

Ad Gentes (Decree on the Mission Activity of the Church)

This growing sense of awareness began receiving official support in Roman Catholic circles with *Ad Gentes* (Decree on the Mission Activity of the Church) in 1965. It was the first document from an Ecumenical Council which was devoted specifically to the Church's missionary activity and it represented a radical rethinking of the meaning of the Church's mission in the changing world. It also established evangelisation as one of the fundamental missions of *all* the members of the Catholic Church – not just the Church in the developing world.

Evangelii Nuntiandi ("Evangelisation in the Modern World")

In 1974, the Third Ordinary Synod of Bishops focused on "evangelisation" and made it an urgent priority for the Church throughout the world. Suddenly, a word scarcely used in the documents of Vatican II became the focus for this international gathering of bishops.

Blessed Pope Paul VI produced his ground-breaking encyclical, *Evangelii Nuntiandi*, in 1975. Theologians and missionaries regard this encyclical as one of the great works to influence and challenge the modern Church. It has shaped and inspired the entire evangelising activity of the Church, including Pope Francis' apostolic exhortation of 2013, *Evangelii Gaudium* ("The Joy of the Gospel").

The synod and the subsequent document, *Evangelii Nuntiandi*, started a new movement in the Church. If the Church is essentially missionary, every Christian has a duty to bear witness to Christ despite being in widely differing cultural and social contexts.

The synod highlighted two important thrusts to evangelisation today. Both need a special and tailored approach:

- taking the Gospel to places where it has never been heard (**primary evangelisation**)
- taking the Gospel to places where it was once strong but has now been obscured or has disappeared altogether (**secondary evangelisation** or **re-evangelisation**).

In the following chapters, we will see how many of the topics raised in this document are still on the agenda today for anyone interested in evangelisation and mission.

The task of evangelisation

The task of evangelisation is an ongoing process. If we are true to a real dynamic in the understanding of Christianity today, culture and history must be *unpacked* to help people in the continuing task of evangelisation. Prior to Vatican II, the Church viewed evangelisation as teaching people information about God, the world and themselves. This didactic approach was good as far as it went but what it left out was the application of our God-given rational capacity to uncover truths for ourselves.

That understanding began to shift its emphasis: we began to speak of revelation in more personal terms. In the 1950s, Karl Rahner was teaching that God reveals *himself* rather than ideas about himself.

At the same time as Rahner, Bernard Lonergan was exploring human experience rather than the mind as the place where God does this revealing. In this newer understanding, revelation was conceived as the offer of God's very self to people by means of concrete actions and symbols in history and in the daily lives of people; faith was understood as a personal response, a self-gift of a person to God.

Dei Verbum (Decree on Divine Revelation)

In Vatican II's *Dei Verbum* (Decree on Divine Revelation), the nature of revelation was seen to be broader than just a set of propositions. In *Dei Verbum* (DV 2), we read that God, in infinite love, speaks to human beings as friends and enters into their lives, so as to invite and receive them into relationship with himself.

> *"To evangelise is to make known the Good News of Jesus Christ and it is about sharing our personal experience of it"*

Encounters with God in the sacraments

It is up to us to ensure that people can understand that encounters with God in Jesus continue to take place in our world. They take place through the sacraments – through the poured water of baptism, in the remembering of the Christian community gathered around the table with bread and wine, in oil given for healing or as a sign of vocation, in gestures of forgiveness or commissioning. The sacraments are concentrated ritual moments that point beyond themselves.

In these ritual moments, Christ offers a loving gesture which brings about a response of love in us. They help us become capable of encountering God in a trusting and loving surrender. Edward Schillebeeckx (*Christ the Sacrament of Encounter with God*) has a good suggestion. If we think of what one human glance, one human smile, can do in our lives we realise how such a smile in a moment can turn us into a new person. In the strength of the love that comes to us, in that small token, we can begin life anew, apparently with powers that were not there before. Therefore, should we not be able to conceive how a smile of the man Jesus, God's smile, how the God-man's glance at us, can change our whole life?

And, if we accept that the sacraments are the God-man's expression of love, imagine what the consequences of that are.

What about those with little overt connection to the Church?

The person of Christ, the depth of the Christian message never fails to be attractive. The opportunities are there to proclaim the riches of grace and love contained in the faith to people with little overt connection to the Church. Opportunities arise in a special and indeed significant way at "historic" moments in people's lives, in the people they are connected to, in the historic life of the community at baptisms, First Holy Communion, weddings and funerals.

Psychoanalyst Erik Erikson is known for his theory on the psychosocial development of human beings. He says that these "historic" moments are related to a continuing, and sometimes repeated, series of points of growth,

"Christ has no body now but yours. No hands, no feet on earth but yours. Yours are the eyes through which he looks compassion on this world. Yours are the feet with which he walks to do good. Yours are the hands through which he blesses all the world. Yours are the hands, yours are the feet, yours are the eyes, you are his body. Christ has no body now on earth but yours"

St Teresa of Ávila

as individuals become more aware of their identity. So, for example, the birth of a child is an event which needs to be named in the life history of that child, of the parents, the extended family, and so on. The birth of the child also marks a profound shift in the relationship of the parents (especially for the first child). Indeed, some unmarried couples (who previously showed no interest in getting married before) decide to marry as a result of becoming parents.

The two primary transitions in human life are birth and death. They govern our moments of existence and our significance. Existence and meaning are inseparable and are acknowledged through rites. And, when we face these transitions, we are dealing with life's meanings for individuals and for their human contexts – family, relations, friends and society in general. We acknowledge the importance of some sort of closing ritual around death and departure (which seems widely unquestioned).

So, why turn to the Church?

Rituals help us express our thoughts and feelings about life's most important events. Birthday parties, for example, honour the passing of another year of life; weddings publicly affirm the love shared by two people; infant baptisms welcome children into the Christian family. The symbolism expressed by a birthday cake, wedding rings and christening gowns all symbolise the important transitions and commitments in life.

A funeral helps us express our beliefs, thoughts and feelings about the death of someone we loved. It helps us continue the relationship we have with the person who has died through our memories of them. In our search for meaning, we believe that the Church can offer help. In their grief and their need to make sense of it all, those who are non-practising may be unable to express what they want from the Church. The Church's rituals offer them hope and, in asking for them, they are asking for God's blessing.

Making the most of this "key moment"

By using our understanding and experience of material things of the world, we express our spiritual thoughts. Christ is the mediator between God's love and us.

Christ's mediation takes place through human acts, through loving and saving acts which find their full expression in expressive and loving gestures. The words of St Teresa of Ávila on the opposite page come to mind.

I hope that you will be convinced of this deep observation in what you find on the pages of this book, that the encounters I describe are rich in potential; but they require an awareness and sensitivity on our part to the possibilities inherent within them.

The following chapters include stories and ideas to help us see how and when we encounter Jesus and how we can help others to encounter him through us.

Before we proceed, we will begin the next chapter with a look at the model Jesus gave us when he met the disciples on the road to Emmaus.

Points for reflection and discussion

- Spend some time reflecting on and remembering the goodness of God in your life.
- Think of some of the "key moments" in your life and what part God played in them.
- If you accept that the sacraments are the God-man's expression of love, imagine what consequences that has for you.

CHAPTER TWO

THE DISCIPLES ENCOUNTER JESUS

The story of the disciples on the road to Emmaus

Luke tells the story about Jesus encountering two of the disciples on the road to Emmaus (Luke 24:13-35). I like Tom Groome's commentary on the story in *Christian Religious Education – Sharing Our Story and Vision*. I will use it as the basis of what happens when we encounter others on their journey.

> The story goes that on the first Easter Sunday, two of Jesus' follower were making their way to Emmaus, a small village about seven miles from Jerusalem. As they went their way, they discussed "all that had happened" (v. 14) over the previous days, and, as might be expected, it was a "lively exchange" (v. 15). Who should join them but the risen Jesus, who began "to walk along with them" (v. 15). For whatever reason, they were "restrained from recognising him" (v. 16). He entered into their company by inquiring, "What are you discussing along your way?" (v. 15). Somewhat distressed and a little impatient at the stranger's ignorance, they wondered where he had been. Surely, everyone in Jerusalem knew "the things that went on there during these past few days?" (v. 18). Rather than seizing this obvious opportunity to disclose his identity (after all, who knew better than he what had gone on there?), he inquired, "What things?" (v. 19). They told him the story as they knew it and their dwindling hope that "he was the one who would set Israel free" (v. 21). Now, adding confusion to their disappointment, "some women" (v. 22) of the group were spreading the "astonishing news" (v. 22) that "he was alive" (v. 23).
>
> Jesus cajoled them for not looking at these recent events within a broader context, and in response to their story and hope, he told them an older *story* and a larger *vision*. "Beginning then, with Moses and all the prophets, he interpreted for them every passage of scripture, which referred to him" (v. 27). He pointed out that the Messiah had to "undergo all this so as to enter into his glory" (v. 26). Surely, now they would recognise him. They did not, and he continued to resist telling them. But he had obviously aroused their curiosity, for they "pressed him" (v. 29) to stay the night in their company. He agreed.

"At table that evening, he blessed and broke bread for them" (v.30) and "with that their eyes were opened and they recognised him; whereupon he vanished from their sight" (v. 31). Then the pieces of their puzzle fell in place, and they remembered how their hearts had "burned" (v. 32) inside them as he talked "on the road" (v. 32). But instead of spending time in self-reproach for not seeing sooner, they set out immediately for Jerusalem (a hazardous journey by night) to tell "the Eleven and the rest of the company" (v. 33). They told the story of what had happened "on the road" and "how they had come to know him in the breaking of the bread" (v. 35).

Luke tells us that while the disciples talk about the recent events, Jesus himself draws near and walks by their side (24:15-16) and enters into conversation with them. Before a word is exchanged before the two parties, we are told that the disciples do not recognise Jesus. He is present to them as a fellow traveller; he is not yet present to the disciples as Lord.

Notice in his encounter with the disciples on the road to Emmaus Jesus doesn't tell the disciples who he is; he listens to them telling him the story of what had happened from their perspective and from their own experience – all the hopes and expectations they'd had, and how confused they were now. They were going in the wrong direction! Jesus wanted them to stay in Jerusalem to witness and, yet, it doesn't stop him from joining them.

As they walk, Jesus recalls for them a larger story of which their story is a part and a vision beyond their vision. He interprets for them "every passage of scripture which referred to him" (24:27). He pointed out that the Messiah had to "undergo all this so as to enter into his glory" (24:26). But, Jesus's explanation is not enough for the disciples to recognise him! The only effect it had was to make their hearts burn (24:32).

Jesus had to do something more, something new to help them. "When he was at table with them, he took bread, blessed and broke it, and gave it to them. Then their eyes were opened, and they recognised him" (24:30-31). The breaking of the bread had an immediate effect and it finally led to the eye-opening of the disciples. Notice that at no point does Jesus tell them *what* to see; he waits for them to come to see for themselves. He doesn't ask them *why* they don't recognise him; he waits for them to recognise him. He doesn't give up on them; he stays with them – helping them to see what is happening.

"Reflecting on our experiences of encountering Jesus and interpreting the experiences is an important part of what we are helping people to do"

In his famous painting of the supper at Emmaus (below), Caravaggio has chosen a dramatic moment to represent what was happening at the table that night. You can see the intensity of emotions of the disciples conveyed by their expressions and gestures. This is because what we actually experience in any happening depends upon the meaning we perceive in that happening.

This perceived meaning is partially discovered in the event and partially imposed on it by our interpretation, for we inevitably interpret whatever happens to us.

Among the experiences each of us has, some key experiences carry more meaning than others and, therefore, influence the meaning we give all our experiences. Some of these key experiences are

extraordinary – like the disciples encountering Jesus on the road to Emmaus. Others are just a part of our ordinary life.

Reflecting on our experiences of encountering Jesus and interpreting the experiences is an important part of what we are helping people to do. They, in turn, often help us to notice where and when we are encountering Jesus too.

On the red dirt road to Mua

My son and I were visiting our White Father friend, Julian Kasiya, in Malawi in the summer of 1994. I was having a much-needed break from a demanding job as a manager in a law firm in the City. Julian had just said Mass in a local village and we were on our way back to where we were staying when we saw some children doing their laundry in a river. Photography is one of my hobbies and I asked if we could stop and take pictures of them.

Two of the boys came up to where the car was parked on the dusty red dirt road and asked if they could sit in the car. They'd never sat in one before, they said. My son asked them what else they hadn't experienced – if they had running water and electricity or if they had television or a telephone, and they hadn't any of them. They asked him, though, if he had ever done his laundry in the river or if he'd ever bathed in a river or tasted sugar from the cane. They were delighted that I wanted to photograph them.

It was not until I was thinking about this conversation and the photographs we had taken during our trip that I realised the importance of the brief encounter I'd had with those boys that day. I was, I thought, a success. I was earning a lot of money, my son was in a very good boarding school, I had a lovely house with a beautiful garden, a housekeeper and a gardener and I was driving a good car. I was, however, not happy; and, when I looked at those boys, I realised that, although I thought I had "everything" and that these boys had "nothing", I had got it the wrong way around.

I wanted what those boys had; I wanted to be happy. I don't know their names and I never saw them again, but my brief encounter with them changed my life. By the time I returned to England, I knew I didn't want to do my job any more. I didn't know what I wanted to do; but I knew it was not that. So, I left my job in the City in search of the pearl of great price that Jesus talks about in Matthew 13.

I decided to take a six-month sabbatical to do nothing, but everyone told me this was out of character for me. A White Father called Aylward Shorter, who was the principal at the Missionary Institute London (MIL) asked if I might like to attend some theology classes at the MIL to give my week a little structure – to have something to do two or three mornings a week. Theology was not something I'd ever thought of studying; but I took his suggestion and before long, I found myself studying theology with the advice and support of some of the students and their rector, Andre Schaminee.

Chapter Two: The disciples encounter Jesus

ENCOUNTERS OF EVANGELISATION 25

CHAPTER THREE

MOST OF JESUS' MINISTRY TOOK PLACE OUT IN THE OPEN

When you take account of the public life of Jesus, most of it took place out in the open; only a fraction of his ministry took place in the Temple or the synagogue. The entire Passion narrative, for example, takes place outside and, even today, the Stations of the Cross on the Via Dolorosa are outside and it is only when you come to the Holy Sepulchre that the Passion moves indoors.

Meeting Jesus in the car park

Tom Grufferty (*The Tablet*, 19 March 2016) tells the story of how he was approached just after Christmas one year by someone saying that, for the first time, she had met Jesus in the parish car park. Grufferty is a parish priest in a pastoral area that consists of six parishes in Portsmouth where they had been running a "welcome home" campaign.

Catholics were being encouraged to invite a Catholic friend, relative or neighbour who was no longer active in the Church to "come home for Christmas" and this woman was one of the people who had been personally invited to come to Mass. Since reports of larger numbers at Mass were most encouraging across all six communities, they had planted their most gifted people to use their charismatic charm in welcoming everyone into the car park on their way into Mass.

But the car park is not always the place to meet Jesus

Self-important people in the parish who are given authority to be stewards can also stop us from encountering Jesus in the car park and in the Church.

I arrived for the Holy Thursday celebration of the Lord's Supper one year, only to find that they had just closed the parish car park. Since I am disabled and I cannot walk more than a few metres, I pleaded with the steward to let me in. I could see that there were still places where I could safely park and I explained to him that I would be unable to come to the Mass if I couldn't park in the car park. I explained that I thought I had given myself plenty of time; but, with his new-found power, this man was immovable. (This could, of course, have been a moment of evangelisation if the right person had been in the position to welcome me in the car park. It's certainly worth a note to appoint the right people for the ministry of welcome.)

I went home feeling very upset and angry at the contradiction I had been confronted with. The Mass of Holy Thursday focuses on how we are called to serve one another. When, in my parish, we present the holy oils that have been blessed at the Cathedral earlier that day (or earlier in the week), we pray:

- with the oil of the sick – and we remember the many people who are sick and those doctors, nurses, family members who look after us when we are sick
- with the oil of catechumens – and we remember the catechists and the catechumens they are preparing for their baptism
- with the oil of chrism – and we remember those who will be anointed when they are confirmed or ordained.

I reflected on how, that night, we remember how Jesus washed the feet of disciples and how this reminds us that we are called to serve one another. If this steward had understood his role as a call to serve people rather than to have power over them, it could have been an opportunity for him to reach out to someone afflicted. Of course, when this kind of thing happens, it highlights the importance of appointing people who understand the role of service. It highlights how we should all be prepared in humility and grace, guided by prayers and sacraments, to be ready to evangelise, to dig deep and act with the kindness that our Lord Jesus asks us to show to everyone.

Jesus cannot be locked in the tabernacle

Tom Grufferty maintains that we have lost that important and crucial aspect of the life of Jesus in our time – telling us that Jesus cannot be locked in the tabernacle nor can he be confined to our churches. On Ash Wednesday of 2016, a group of twelve people in his parish took a daring initiative. They decided to distribute blessed ashes to the general public for two hours after the parish Mass on Ash Wednesday morning.

The group received a most encouraging response from the public. In the two hours more than thirty-five people asked for ashes. Those who received them ranged from churchgoers of all denominations to lapsed Catholics and atheists. They included many people of different ethnic minorities. One woman was complimentary to the group for having the courage to witness publicly to being Christian. Grufferty and his team were taken aback by how quickly people poured out their troubles; three people who were suffering from major bereavements in their lives asked them to pray for them, which suggests that there is a need for a prayer ministry in public places.

The venture was not all plain sailing, as they did receive some outright refusals, which emphasised the importance of having the support of the group. The net result was that they took a risk, as Jesus often did. If we are alert to meeting Jesus in the great world outside our churches, we will find him in the most unexpected people and places. The Incarnation means he is taking part in everything. Jesus is in the street far, far more than we think.

Jesus was in the street in his time too

Jesus doesn't come on demand; he normally comes when we least expect to have an encounter with him. We read in the story of the man born blind that, as Jesus walked along, he saw a man who had been blind since birth (John 9:1-41). We don't know if any conversation took place with the man before Jesus made some mud and smeared it on the man's eyes. Then he said, "Go and wash off the mud in the pool of Siloam," which the man did and when he washed it off, he could see.

"Jesus doesn't come on demand; he normally comes when we least expect to have an encounter with him"

We don't hear the blind man asking to be cured and he was not prepared for what life held in store for him next. The fact that he could see meant that he had lost his livelihood and his place in society. His parents didn't even want anything to do with him. We know that he could no longer beg and we are not told how he goes on to make a living for himself. All we know is that he got something he wasn't asking for. He gained physical and spiritual insight and he was persecuted for it by the leaders of the time.

Living out the compassion of Jesus

Daniel O'Leary, in his book, *Already Within*, tells the story of a woman who left a message on his answerphone, saying, "Sir, I would like to have my baby christened next Sunday." He tensed up; the woman didn't even know his name – and nor was she aware of the parish's requirement of "two months' notice" or the need for the pre-baptismal talks. He fumed for a while and then called her back saying that it was not as easy as she thought to have a baby baptised and he invited her round the next week so he could fill her in on a few matters. "No," she replied, "you'd better come around here!"

This he did, his shield and spear at the ready and in indignant mode. After all, rules are rules. There are diocesan regulations to be honoured; you can't just go around baptising everything that moves like we used to, he thought. It was due to the mistake of doing this in the past that only a fraction of Catholics practise their faith now.

Daniel found the young mother's face discoloured. She was just out of hospital after a bad beating at the hands of her boyfriend. There was a sadness in her voice. Looking into the cot with great love, and a sudden smile, she told him that she did not want what had happened to her ever to happen to her baby. She thought she would feel safe in our Church. After talking a while, Daniel's heart melted. He promised to do what she wanted, to make it as easy as possible for her to protect her little girl from whatever threatened her fragile presence in a precarious world.

Another priest told Daniel a similar story. When he, also slightly affronted by a brusque phone call, went around to the house, the mother explained to him that she had fought tooth and nail to bring her child to full term, in spite of the pressures and threats of her boyfriend, and even of her own Catholic family, to have an abortion.

The two priests compared notes about how suddenly their approaches had changed and how ashamed they had felt at their self-righteousness and ego-hurt. Their brief encounters with these two women helped them to see how far they had drifted from the compassion of Jesus. Daniel says that such experiences in a priest's life can help lead them to try different ways of looking at their role as pastoral, non-judgemental servants of God. (*See* Daniel O'Leary, *Already Within* (Dublin: Columba Press, 2007), 56-57).

Perspective shift

The two priests just mentioned experienced a shift of perspective in their attitudes. Priests are not the only ones who sometimes need to experience this kind of change; this is something we all have to do from time to time. Here is a story about a man leaving his work late one evening in the City that will further our understanding of the notion of a perspective shift.

As the story goes, the man is tired. He bought a newspaper to read on the train home and thought, "At least I'll get a seat on the train and it will be quiet." After a couple of stops, however, a father entered his car on the train with two young children. The man sat in his seat staring out of the window and the two children ran up and down the train car disturbing everyone. The man became more and more irritated with the father and, finally, he asked him, "Do you not realise that your children are bothering everyone?" The father looked at him sadly and said, "We have just come from the hospital where their mother died unexpectedly and they don't know how to react to what's happened." The man's attitude underwent a transformation; he changed from being irritated by this father to feeling compassion for him. Nothing else had changed. The children were still disturbing everyone; but the man saw the situation from a completely different perspective.

If we are to be willing to reach out to those who do not share our faith or those living a different lifestyle from ours, those who are asking something of us, there will be times when all of us need to make that kind of perspective shift. Our willingness to do so will make a big difference in the way we respond and how Christ-like we can be in the circumstances.

Chapter Three: Most of Jesus' ministry took place out in the open

Points for reflection and discussion

- Is there a time when you experienced a perspective shift in your understanding?
- Think of a time when you encountered Jesus somewhere unexpectedly.
- Think of a time and place when you helped someone else encounter Jesus.

Volunteers bring the presence of Christ into people's lives

The Archbishop of Birmingham, Bernard Longley, volunteered alongside members of the city's Sikh, Catholic and Muslim communities at a soup kitchen for homeless people in January 2017. In an interview on the Birmingham Diocese website, he said that the volunteers "are truly bringing the presence of Christ into people's lives".

Figures show that there are currently 2,800 people in Birmingham officially listed as homeless, of whom a growing number are living on the streets. When temperatures plummet across the city, the practical assistance and compassionate support offered by volunteers at the soup kitchen every night of the year is a lifeline to those in need.

The Archbishop said it was good to see how the Catholic volunteers co-operate on this city corner with

other generous volunteers in caring for so many needy people in the city.

Pupils from a local middle school make the sandwiches for the twice-monthly soup kitchen and a primary school recently raised money to accommodate a homeless couple who had been living in a tent for more than a year over the Christmas period. Other Catholic schools donate their Lenten and Advent collections to the running costs of the soup kitchen and the annual Christmas party for homeless men and women which brings together nearly two hundred people from across the city of Birmingham.

The number of homeless men has increased in the last five years and even more young men have recently been presenting as homeless in the last twelve months. Those who are experiencing homelessness for the very first time really struggle.

The Archdiocese of Birmingham, with the help of other Catholic partners, is trying to do its bit. It has recently opened a place of refuge in Birmingham for vulnerable female asylum seekers who have no recourse to public funds, called Fatima House. In April 2017, it will also open Tabor House, an emergency shelter for homeless men and women in Birmingham.

In his Angelus address on 9 January 2017, Pope Francis urged Catholics to practically and prayerfully support the homeless. He asked for prayers for all those living and dying on the streets, as freezing conditions swept across Europe. The Vatican itself runs three hostels close to St Peter's and to Termini train station. As the weather becomes cold, they remain open twenty-four hours a day. In addition, a number of Vatican cars are dotted across the city as places to sleep for those who wish to remain on the streets.

Volunteers elsewhere can to do their bit too

Several charities link up a number of the Christian Churches in the UK. Their aim is to provide hot food, accommodation, company and real advice and guidance to around a dozen homeless guests a night during the worst of the winter months in the UK. Thanks to contributions by parishioners and grants they can apply for, they can buy the necessary mattresses, bedding and other equipment to host the shelter in each of the churches in the charity. The quality of the clothes and food they are being offered is first class. The participating churches say they get more help than they need.

We can ignore the issue of homelessness on our doorstep, saying it's nothing to do with us – it's the job of the government. Supporting the homeless, however, in such prayerful and practical ways gives our parish and local communities a positive way to live our Christian call to reach out to those without homes or shelter.

Points for reflection and discussion
- Investigate what is being done in your parish/locality for the homeless.
- In what way do you live out the compassion of Jesus?
- Think of someone who lives their life as a pastoral, non-judgemental servant of God.

Chapter Three: Most of Jesus' ministry took place out in the open

CHAPTER FOUR

ABOUT WELCOMING

Remember the story of Abraham

We read in Genesis that the Lord appeared to Abraham in the heat of the day as he sat at the entrance of his tent. He saw three strangers approaching him; he ran to meet them, bowed down in greeting, sat them down in comfort in a shady spot, provided all their needs, hovered nearby while they ate, listening to their stories, then went with them to set them on their way (Genesis 18:1-16).

Abraham does not recognise the Lord; all he sees is three travellers who are weary and thirsty as they come in off the desert where temperatures often reach up to 50° C. He greets the central figure with the words, "my lord" – the common language of courtesy used. It doesn't mean that he realised that this was "the Lord". In the *New Revised Standard Version (NRSV)* of the Bible, the word "lord" is not capitalised – illustrating the point that Abraham's offer of food, rest and water shows he had no idea who he was entertaining. Some say they were angels in human bodies.

Many centuries later, the letter to the Hebrews (13:2) reminds us: "Do not neglect to show hospitality to strangers for by doing that some have entertained angels without knowing it." Imagine if we were to greet every stranger we meet in this way – especially those who come to join us for Mass.

Catholic means "welcoming everyone"

Technically, the word "catholic" comes from two Greek words: *kata* (meaning "according to" or "throughout") and *holos* (meaning "whole"); in Latin this became *catholicus*, "universal"; in that sense the Church is for everyone and it needs to welcome everyone.

Not all of our parishes are all that welcoming to many, and some are still learning how to be welcoming. The list of those who don't feel welcome is long. It is worth asking how we welcome newcomers and visitors, people who are on their own, those from travelling families or those who are single parents, those who are separated or divorced and remarried, gay, lesbian or transgendered, those with learning disabilities, those from ethnic minorities, or seeking refugee or asylum status. That assumes, of course, that we know who they are and that they are there (even if they are only occasionally there).

It is also worth noticing how we welcome parishioners who regularly worship with us. My mother died a couple of years ago at the age of ninety-three. Right up to the time she died, she went to church every Sunday morning. It was one of the high points in her week; she appreciated feeling that she belonged to the parish community and that people were pleased to see her each week. Parishes can learn from and care for older people, benefiting from their gifts. Leeds Diocese has just published a guide for parishes on how to welcome older people (*see* www.growingoldgracefully.org.uk).

In a similar way, families with young children benefit from feeling welcome and from the experience of being part of the parish community.

The Church must be for everyone, welcoming and accompanying

Sheila Keefe (*Pastoral Review*, March-April, 2007) looked into the question of the Church being welcoming and accompanying. She has worked with the Catholic Bishops' Conference of England and Wales at parish, diocesan and national level on this subject. She makes the point that many of the groups we've mentioned have special welcoming needs which must be addressed if they are to be fully integrated into parish life.

Sheila was part of a working party called "Everybody's Welcome" that looked at what was needed at parish, diocesan and national level to open up our churches to all-comers. They emphasised the need for Catholics to understand the challenges people face – and, in respect of people in that list of people who don't feel welcome – Catholics need to know what help and support is needed from their parishes and where that help can be found.

Since his election, Pope Francis repeatedly reminds us that the Church must be for everyone, welcoming and accompanying. In his apostolic exhortation *Amoris Laetitia* ("The Joy of Love") he calls all of us in the Roman Catholic Church to be more welcoming and less judgemental.

Communication is "key"

The Everybody's Welcome working party encourages every parish to have:

- the times of Mass clearly displayed
- a welcome committee
- a mission statement
- a website
- welcome leaflets at the back of church with details and contact points for parish activities
- photos of PPC (parish pastoral council) members
- a loop system and disabled access to the church, the confessional and the WC; in addition, there should be access to the lectern for disabled readers and for disabled people to receive Holy Communion and, as extraordinary ministers, to distribute it
- books and quiet toys for children
- coffee after Mass

- welcome parties for newcomers
- car parking facilities
- open churches during the week
- lifts to Mass.

This kind of communication is key to ensure that everyone feels they belong, that they are welcome.

Those elusive extra ingredients

These are all excellent ideas but for the recipe to be successful, two extra ingredients are needed. Firstly, there are legal, safeguarding and insurance issues involved in offering people lifts that must be complied with. Secondly, there must be a will and a way for us to reach out to people we don't know and to welcome them into the heart of our community. Sheila says that she remembers going to Mass on holiday and being impressed by a mission statement, prominently displayed on the wall of the church, which said, "Our aim is to welcome everyone who comes to this church." But when she came out of church not a single person approached her or even made eye contact!

Additional "welcome tips"

Some of the Everybody's Welcome working party top tips for busy parishes include these suggestions:

On talking in church

"Invite everyone at Mass on Sunday to speak afterwards to someone they don't know or haven't spoken to before." Now if people complain that there's too much talking in the church before Mass begins and it disturbs their prayer, people could come into church in silence and talk after Mass is finished. Of course, it is important to be respectful and considerate to those who have remained in the church after Mass for prayer. A friend of mine told me about a sign in Spain, which he translated as:

> Before Mass, we talk to God.
> At Mass, God talks to us.
> After Mass, we talk to each other!

Making visitors especially welcome

The priest might welcome everyone and then invite the people to welcome the person sitting next to them. The Bishops' Conference website quotes one person, who said:

> I felt really awkward going to Midnight Mass at Christmas with my partner's family, because I am not a Catholic. The first thing the priest did was to welcome all the visitors, especially those who are not Catholics. It made such a difference.

Another quote is from a woman who said that she only went to Mass that first time to accompany a friend who had come to stay for the weekend. She said:

> The experience was amazing: from the greeting at the door and the canon's welcome to visitors from a variety of places (which he named), I felt

an extraordinary welcome and throughout Mass there was a feeling of being in a family and surrounded by love strong enough to make me feel greatly moved and tearful. I went back alone the next week and the next and the next and every time I felt the same emotions. Shortly afterwards I joined the RCIA group. I feel that the Church is now my other family.

Name badge Sunday

It's very unusual for family members not to know one another's names. But how many of us can name all those who worship with us in God's family each Sunday? It's even more of a challenge if people are new to a parish or are not regulars at a particular church. Name badges are an accepted feature of meetings where participants are not assumed to know one another. So as one of our top tips, we suggest that parishes choose one (or more) Sunday when everyone attending Mass will be invited to wear a name badge.

Safeguarding protocols in parishes must always be borne in mind. The parish pastoral council (PPC)

"The letter to the Hebrews (13:2) reminds us: 'Do not neglect to show hospitality to strangers for by doing that some have entertained angels without knowing it.' Imagine if we were to greet every stranger we meet in this way – especially those who come to join us for Mass"

members or parish welcomers might invite parishioners individually to coffee after Mass on those Sundays, calling them by their name. The badges will also enable personal invitations to parishioners to parish events.

Organise home visits

Priests no longer visit the homes of everyone in the parish; they, like families, are often too stretched now to do more than visit the housebound and those most urgently in need. In many places parishioners have realised their shared responsibility for visiting; it is a simple yet effective means of building up the parish community.

Portsmouth Diocese has developed a ministry for lay people to do home visits called "Keeping In Touch". You can download a copy at www.kit4catholics.org.uk. Establishing this ministry will require training and support for volunteers, including safeguarding clearance, so contact your safeguarding coordinator for advice if necessary.

These are ideas which have been used and have worked, but again, that elusive, extra ingredient could still be missing. The bottom line, without which no "tip" will succeed, is that we dare to reach out and touch the life of the stranger in our midst. Remember what Jesus said: "I was a stranger and you welcomed me" (Matthew 25:35).

A culture change

A culture change is taking place in the Church, and we are finding ways to broaden our ways of being Catholic in today's Church.

> **Ask yourself:**
> - When do you feel welcome? Is it when someone smiles at you or when they strike up a conversation with you, perhaps to introduce themselves or to make a comment, however general, about the weather, for example?
> - When did you last make an effort to make someone welcome?

No special skills needed

We don't need special training to do what we could already be doing in our everyday lives, when we care for our parents and children, when we visit our friends, listen to their stories and support them in their times of trial or difficulty, when we help one another at work, when we look to the future with hope and confidence, even when we smile at passers-by. All that is needed is that extra bit of God-given courage to do for the stranger what we can do so well for family and friend. It would cost so little for us all (not just the official welcomers and ushers) to welcome and greet those who approach our bench looking for a space, say a prayer for them, provide them with hymn books and Mass sheets, help the elderly to stand and sit, point out the children's books, WCs and loop system if appropriate. We quickly discern if they want to be left alone. Some do and it is important to respect that, but many respond with smiles and gratitude and immediately feel welcomed and valued.

What is more important is that, at the end of Mass, the majority of people, once spoken to, are really eager to talk. It helps if we have something prepared to say such as, "I don't know you; my name is", or to make a comment about their children, the service, the hymns, the notices or, failing all else, the weather!

All of us need welcome. All of us are strangers in a sense, pilgrims and exiles journeying to the Promised Land, to the home and happiness we seek throughout our lives.

> **Points for reflection and discussion**
> - How welcoming is your parish?
> - How welcoming are you personally?
> - Has what Sheila Keefe said challenged you to dare to reach out and touch the life of the stranger in your midst?

The Church should welcome everyone – even those with challenging behaviour

The difficulties that can arise because of challenging behaviour is highlighted in the case of Adam, a 13-year-old boy in America. Dr Jane Shields is the retired director of the National Autistic Society's Early Bird Centre in the USA. She tells the story (*The Tablet*, 21 June 2008) of how a priest in Minnesota acted to get Adam barred from attending Mass after parishioners complained that his behaviour in church was highly disruptive. Adam has autism spectrum disorder (ASD).

His mother, who violated a court order excluding her son from Mass, insists that he was not dangerous. While it is impossible to comment without knowing the full details, what we do know is that teenagers often complain that they are bored during Mass. People with ASD are no different; but, in addition, people with ASD may be distressed by noises or smells, and they get anxious about the proximity of other people.

They are often upset by changes in routine and may react if something different is taking place during Mass. They may be obsessed by a special interest or need to engage in repetitive actions, such as jumping or hand flapping, to relieve anxiety. They may have little or no verbal communication, and therefore have difficulty in sharing their feelings or communicating their needs to others.

Jane says it can be helpful for the person with ASD to have something appropriate to their level of functioning to occupy and distract them during Mass. People with ASD are often visual learners, so visual aids can help them to follow the Mass, to know what is happening and when the Mass will end. Learning about the Mass and learning how to participate in the Mass is a lifelong journey for all of us; parents have to be creative as they travel down the path with their children. Families who have children with autism have to find ways or find help to be more creative.

It is not hard to see both sides of the situation in Minnesota, with the priest's duty to balance the needs of a family against the safety of other parishioners. Society has made a lot of progress in recent years in respecting the rights to inclusion of people with disabilities. These rights include their access to faith and worship settings and communities. Nearly twenty years ago, in 1998, the Bishops' Conference of England and Wales reminded us in the document *Valuing Difference* that God loves us as we are – that the rich diversity of the body of Christ includes those who live with disabilities.

Valuing Difference informs us that our task, as members of the Church, is to translate Christ's message of inclusion into practical action so that the contribution of each member is respected and nurtured. They called this "our shared mission". Legislation has ensured that we consider access for people in wheelchairs, a loop system for the hearing-impaired and large-print Mass books for those with limited vision – but we must not forget autism, the "invisible" disability that affects one in 100 of us (more than 500,000 people in Britain).

People with ASD experience the world in a different way. Their disability is primarily social, affecting social interaction, social communication, and imagination. People with ASD need and enjoy routine. They may show a pattern of narrow, repetitive activity and may develop special interests; they find them calming. Many people with ASD show sensory sensitivities, reacting in unusual ways to stimuli such as sounds, smell, tastes and textures. Their interest often focuses on detail, rather than the overall context. They are poor "mind-readers", and have difficulty in understanding other people.

Some people on the spectrum develop only limited communication. They can be helped by visual systems, such as symbols, and by the people around them simplifying their own use of words. People with ASD may show inappropriate behaviour in response to unpleasant triggers, such as fear or anxiety. Such behaviour is frequently an attempt to communicate their feelings – so, rather than condemn this behaviour, we need to look at its triggers, the possible causes and the results so that we can understand the reason underlying the behaviour and we can anticipate future problems.

All of us are equal in the eyes of God

"How schools meet their equality objectives is of great relevance to eliminate discrimination, harassment and victimisation of people who have disabilities"

All of us are equal in the eyes of God, but it sometimes seems that some are more equal than others in the eyes of the world. How schools meet their equality objectives has been affected by recent disability legislation. This is now a mainstream issue of social awareness and one of great relevance to eliminate discrimination, harassment and victimisation of people who have disabilities.

John McCorkell is an adviser who visits schools all over the UK. Due to a lack of oxygen when he was born, he was diagnosed with cerebral palsy when he was only six months old. His entire right side is affected. His speech is impaired. He cannot walk without the aid of sticks and he has to use a wheelchair. He has not allowed these disabilities to stop him from leading an independent and fulfilling life. When he visits a school, John normally leads a whole school assembly in which he explains to the children the nature of his disabilities, the problems he has faced and the successes he has achieved in overcoming them (including playing wheelchair basketball and gaining two university degrees).

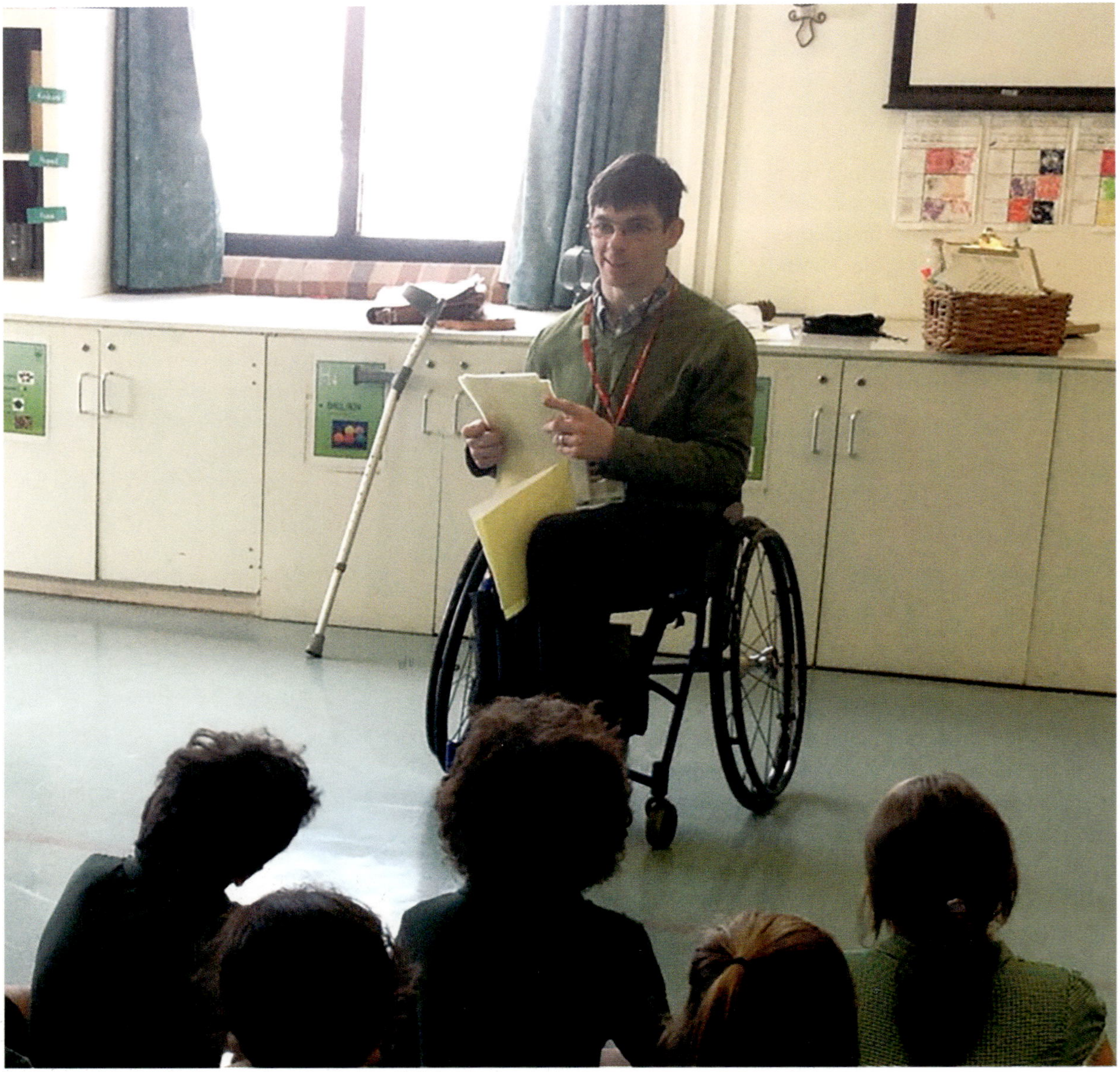

His visits achieve a change in the way that people with disabilities are perceived, which enables the children and young people to understand that any disabled peers they have may do things slightly differently, but perhaps just need a little more time and space to do so. After the assembly, John leads workshops with each individual class, and they take part in practical activities which give them some new and often surprising understanding of what it might be like to be without sight or speech or what it feels like to be in a wheelchair and having to rely on somebody else to wheel them around. They learn about sign language and the need for clear communication – and they learn that disabilities are not always physical. They can be intellectual or emotional.

The Judeo-Christian belief that every person is made in the image and likeness of God and in his eyes is of unique value is based on Genesis 1:27. John reminds Christians not to forget those many people who are disabled in any way and says that we, like the Christ we represent, must discover their dignity and their relationship with God. A change of perception in our traditional approach to disability takes time though, and recent changes in thought and legislation across Europe are just beginning to make significant challenges that enable practical solutions.

Picture Jesus drawing near and accompanying the disciples

Recall how Jesus drew near and accompanied the disciples on their journey. It is a biblical image of God's initiative in the story of revelation which continues to take place today. God enters history and reveals his hidden purpose.

For Luke, two of the clearest distinguishing marks of God's visit of salvation in Jesus are the mission of Jesus in reaching out to people on the fringes of society (Luke 19:10) and his familiarity with them (Luke 7:34).

Points for reflection and discussion
- Debate Adam's story (or reflect on it). Who was right – Adam's mother or the priest?
- If Adam was in your parish, what would you have done? What do you think Jesus would have done?
- Name some people on the fringes of society. Who helps them in your area?

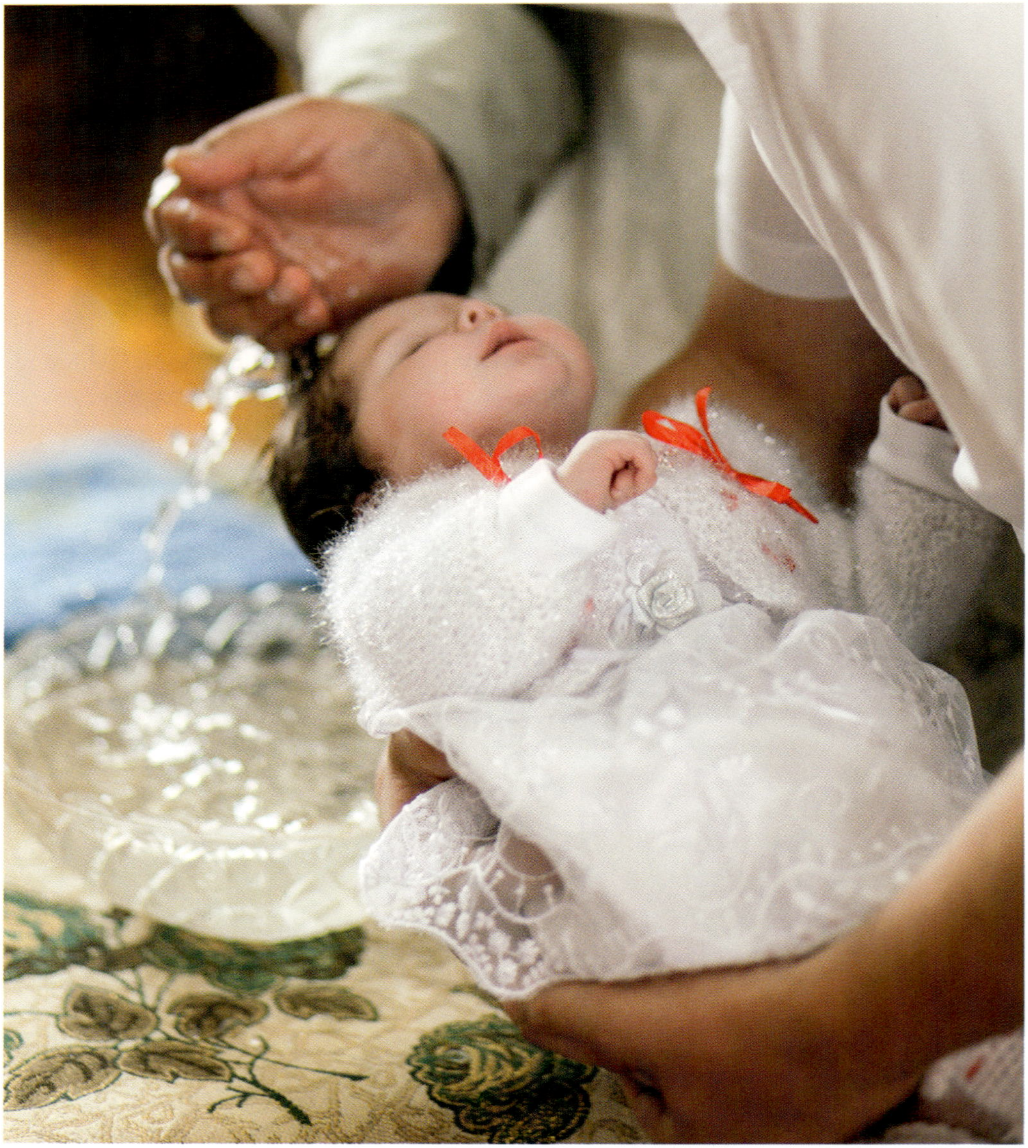

CHAPTER FIVE

BRIEF ENCOUNTERS THROUGH BAPTISMS, WEDDINGS AND FUNERALS

Our focus in this book is on how encounters with Jesus can change us, can evangelise us – can help us to believe that every person is made in the image of God and is of unique value in his eyes and that God loves each of us very much. We will now look at how encounters with Jesus, encounters with God's immense love, can take place at baptisms, weddings and funerals – three occasions when people will approach the Church.

These encounters may take place with the people immediately involved, namely, the families of the one being baptised, getting married or whose funeral it is. On the other hand, they are fertile ground for the friends who come along. They may be Catholics who have distanced themselves from the Church; they may be people of other faiths or of no faith. There are great opportunities of evangelisation available to us in the way we celebrate the liturgies and the way we welcome the people.

Opportunities of evangelisation at baptisms

The baptismal liturgy, with its symbols of water, oil, light and garment, calls into the present the reality of Christ's redeeming work: his dying and rising, his ministry, and the meaning of this for us as members of his Church. Our very use of the word "baptism" – which in Greek means "immersion"– has become a metaphor for our belief that we, by dying in Christ, are immersed into the life of Christ, who is the resurrection and the life.

Pope Leo I compared the natural life of our bodies with the supernatural life of our souls. Baptism, he said, corresponds to our bodily birth. When he baptises infants, a Benedictine friend of mine talks about how babies come to new life in the world when they are born by passing through the waters of their mother's womb; likewise, they are born to new life in baptism by passing through the waters of baptism. This explanation can engage people of all ages and all backgrounds.

Infant baptism

People come to the Church asking to have their children baptised for many reasons. Those who are practising will say that they want their child to be a member of the family of God; they want to give their child the gift of their faith.

Those who are not practising have other reasons. Some of them are being pressurised by their parents (that is, the grandparents of the child to be baptised); some say that they want their child to grow up with good values and they believe they will find them in the Church. Others want their child to have the best start they can give them in life. And, yes, sometimes what they perceive to be the best start is a Catholic school education – and they know that they will not be offered a place unless the child has been baptised.

Some people will want baptism for superstitious reasons with vague notions about what the sacrament means and can offer, hoping baptism will act as a kind of charm of protection for their child. So, what if they ask what happened to limbo? Tell them that although it had become a part of the common teaching of the Church, it was never defined in any Church council or document. The fact that limbo cannot be found anywhere in the current *Catechism* officially confirms that it is not now Church teaching.

> *"This brief encounter the woman had with the priest and with her neighbours ended up changing everything for her"*

The parent(s) may be married, or the parents may be living together. Even if they are regularly practising Catholics, they may not be familiar with the language and rituals of the Church when it comes to the sacrament of baptism (and may feel embarrassed about their ignorance) and they may be nervous. When they are faced with being asked to attend a programme of preparation, they may be diffident. The arrival of a single person to enquire about baptism is always interesting. Is s/he a single parent? Or does the appearance of only one parent (often the mother), evidence nervousness on the part of the couple?

It is essential that the parish priest personally (or others he designates) prepare the parents properly for their infant's baptism. They should know the meaning of this sacrament and the obligations attached to it through pastoral advice, common prayer and bringing several families together and, where possible, visiting them at home (*Code of Canon Law* c. 851 §2).

In my experience, couples are more likely to share issues during this one-to-one meeting when they are on their own territory. They are more likely to say that they are not married, that they married outside the Church or that one of them was married before, so they think they cannot marry in the Church. I've discovered that, in many cases, people have excluded themselves when, in fact, there is a solution to their problem – or there isn't actually a problem. The important thing is that any problems we find should not give us reason to reject these people; on the contrary, welcoming them and helping them to solve these problems is an opportunity to serve them.

These one-to-one meetings with the parent(s) are an opportunity to have a brief encounter with them that rarely presents itself otherwise.

Parish programmes to prepare parents for infant baptism

It is not easy to find a published programme that suits every parish. Ulick Loring (*The Tablet*, 12 May 2012) describes that his parish had been using an extremely dated video from another culture; the quality of the filming and the editing was poor. It depicted a bygone Ireland of the 1970s and the chauvinist depictions of family life made people laugh. Since there was a dearth of materials tailored to the needs of a parish such as theirs, he and the catechists found a creative solution.

The catechists wanted a film set in their own church, so they made a film of a re-enacted baptism in their church. They included stopping points in the film with an explanation of the signs and symbols of the sacrament – and the deeper significance of baptism.

During the rite of baptism, people move from place to place in the church to show how we are on a journey of faith:

- the baptism begins with a welcome outside the church or in the narthex
- the people then enter the church to listen to the reading of scripture
- next, they move to the baptismal font
- finally, they move to the altar.

They planned the film so that it could be paused and the parents invited into discussion during the preparation session. For example, after the portrayal of the greeting outside the church or in the porch, the film could be paused and the parents could be asked what they are asking for. They are asked why they have chosen the name they have given their child and why we make the sign of the cross. During this pause, there could also be a reflection on what it means to belong to Christ.

The film then shows how all the people move into the nave of the church to listen to the reading of scripture. The reason people move from place to place in the church during the rite of baptism is to show how we are on a journey of faith. There is another stopping point here, where the parents can be asked to think about what God might be saying through the readings.

Next, they move to the baptismal font. Parents find it very powerful to reflect on how the waters of baptism bring their child to new life – and how being anointed with chrism will help the child be more like Christ, as well as to take on his mission. The baptism concludes with the family and friends moving to the altar, where this child will eventually receive Holy Communion.

They say the Lord's Prayer – the prayer of our Christian family, a family this child now belongs to.

With more and more people having access to modern technology, parishes can tailor-make their own baptism preparation programmes; they do not have to be dependent on a published programme which may not suit them. Seeing a baptism in a place you are familiar with and with the priest who will be baptising your child makes this film a powerful catechetical tool, which can enhance the encounter between catechist or priest and the parents.

When my son was born

When my son was born, I was not a practising Catholic. I had left the Church about ten years before and had married outside the Church. My father had accepted my choice to marry in the Church of Scotland because my husband's uncle was a minister; he baptised all the babies, blessed all the marriages and buried all the dead in the family. When my son was born, though, it was very different.

My father told me that he wanted Nicholas to be baptised in the Catholic Church – and, although I did not know why, so did I. My father lived in New York City, where I grew up. He was going to come to London to see Nicholas just after he was born, but he died a couple of weeks before he was due to come. Shortly after his funeral, a friend brought me the silver christening cup he was planning to give Nicholas. I can still remember how torn I felt. I wanted to please my father and have Nicholas baptised; but I felt it was hypocritical to ask for him to be baptised in a Church I no longer felt a part of.

Around three years later, Nicholas and I were visiting an old high school friend of mine in upstate New York and she asked me why I had not had him baptised. She said she wanted to be his godmother. I told her how I felt, and said I had been warned that there was no point asking my parish priest to baptise Nicholas; he would not do it unless I started going to Mass regularly – and, at that point, I was not willing to do that. My friend was undeterred; she knew her parish priest well, she called him and asked him to baptise Nicholas during our short visit. Although I was not practising, she told him that I wanted Nicholas to be baptised and that I was a person of strong faith and she knew I would bring Nicholas up as a Catholic if he was baptised. (To this day, I do not know how she could have been so certain I would do so.)

The next day was the priest's birthday; he was celebrating Mass at midday and, to my surprise, he said he would baptise Nicholas after the Mass. He invited the people who were at Mass to stay for the baptism; and, more than thirty-five years later, I can still remember the joyful and warm welcome we received.

When the priest asked for our address for the baptism register, we discovered that, by some coincidence, he had spent some time just a few hundred metres up the road from our house in London with the Mill Hill

Missionaries a couple of years before. I thanked him for agreeing to baptise Nicholas, and he told me that he had been to my parish in Mill Hill; he said it was a good parish and then he said, "I wonder if God is using me to invite you to come back to the Church, to the sacraments." And, he asked me to think about it.

I was deeply touched by my encounter with this priest and by his willingness to baptise Nicholas without making any demands on me. I am not advocating a ban on preparation sessions for parents of infants to be baptised; but, in my case, I think this was exactly the right approach to take with me. He accepted me just as I was and, looking back, this was my first experience of the unconditional love of God (which would take me several more years to accept).

> **Points for reflection and discussion**
> - Do you think that the coincidence I describe above is more of a "God-incidence"?
> - Have you ever experienced a coincidence like this and, if so, did you recognise God's hand in the incident?
> - Do you believe in the unconditional love of God – as shown by this priest to me?

Older children called to holiness

There are increasing numbers of young people in the seven to fourteen age group who are not only asking the *big* questions about life, but are looking to the Church as a place that provides the answers – and parishes need to be ready to respond to their needs.

A few years ago I met a boy of ten and his eight-year-old sister who wanted to be baptised. Their Muslim father had forbidden their mother to have them baptised when they were born; and, though he had left them, the mother continued to respect his wishes – although she began to take them to Mass and she taught them to pray. The children told me that they wanted to be baptised, to receive Jesus in Holy Communion with everyone else; they wanted to belong – so much so that they contacted their father to ask his permission.

These children are part of a growing number of older children who are coming to the Church asking for baptism. They may have begun to ask the big questions about where they have come from, where they are going, what they are doing here, which lead them to an awareness of God; they may have relatives or friends who go to church. They may have come to church for a baptism, a wedding or a funeral – or, like these children, they may already be coming to Mass, and they want to belong, they want to be like the friends they've made at church.

The Church gives us guidelines about how to initiate these children in Part II of the Rite of Christian Initiation of Adults (RCIA) which includes a section devoted to children in this age group who are asking for baptism. It is called the Christian Initiation of Children of Catechetical Age (CICCA). Just as with adults who are asking for baptism, children's initiation can be extended over several years, if need be, before they receive the sacraments. We are told that the initiation of these children requires both a conversion that is personal and somewhat developed in proportion to their age and, as with adults, their initiation is marked by several steps and liturgical rites.

The process begins with a period of enquiry, an opportunity for the beginnings of faith. It is a time when the children should be encouraged to ask questions and to explore any preconceptions they may have about the Catholic faith. It is a time when they begin to know the person of Jesus Christ.

The children should only move forward to the first step of the process and become catechumens when they are ready to do so – when they express their belief in Jesus and express their intention to respond to him and to follow him. This decision about their readiness will be made in coordination with the parish priest, the catechists and the children's parents.

The same four dynamics of the RCIA that apply to adults belong to the period of the catechumenate with the children and each of those dynamics (or stages) leads to a step on the journey:

- They begin with a time of enquiry – Who is this man, Jesus?
    - ◇ They take their first step and become catechumens when they say they want to follow Jesus.
- There is then a time of getting to know Jesus better, nurtured by prayer and scripture.
    - ◇ Their next step is the celebration of a penitential rite or a scrutiny.
- Then there is a time of reflection centred on conversion, marked by presentations of the Creed and the Lord's Prayer and the preparation for the Sacraments of Initiation.
    - ◇ The last step is the celebration of baptism, confirmation and First Holy Communion.

The CICCA is a time of suitable catechesis – when their faith is nurtured and their conscience is developed in proportion to their age. Their progress will depend on the help and example of their companions and the influence of their parents, godparents, sponsors, catechists and the community. There is the closest connection between what we believe and how we live. We do not first know Jesus and then follow him. Like the disciples, we come to know him by following him. They will spend time learning how to pray and discovering something about living by faith. In many parishes, there is a Liturgy of the Word for children within the Sunday Mass – and participating in it will give children the opportunity to mix with other children of their age.

And, since the Church's life is apostolic, the children and their families are encouraged to work with others in the parish outreach to the poor. A keen social conscience is normally found in children of this age. To join with others of their own age group in activities – such as packing food parcels for the elderly and poor at Christmas, preparing sandwiches for homeless people, engaging in fundraising for the Catholic charity CAFOD or local hospices or parish projects abroad – helps them not only to make new friends but gives them a sense of purpose to their lives.

Doctrine is what the Church believes and teaches – and the doctrine included in the CICCA should be sufficient and appropriate to the age of the children. The teaching of the Church unfolds in history and it will unfold gradually in the life of these children.

Rite of Christian Initiation of Adults (RCIA)

Bishop Brian Noble told a story of a woman he called "the bingo queen". She was a person of no faith but she came to his parish religiously every week when he was a young priest to play bingo. When her husband died, her bingo friends supported her through her bereavement and, shortly afterwards, she asked if she could become a Catholic. She wanted to be like the people who had reached out to her in her grief.

All types of people come to the Church to enquire about becoming Catholic. People who are searching for a meaning in their lives come and people who are in some way dissatisfied with their lives and want something *more* come. Some are married to a Catholic; perhaps they have been coming to Mass for years and years and, finally, someone asked them if they would like to become Catholic. Some have met the Church through a baptism or a First Communion or a confirmation. Some have been to a wedding and something was said that suddenly made sense for them. Some have met the Church through someone who was sick; or, perhaps, they met the Church at a funeral. Others have met Christians at work or next door and wondered why they are like they are – and decided to enquire into what this Church is about.

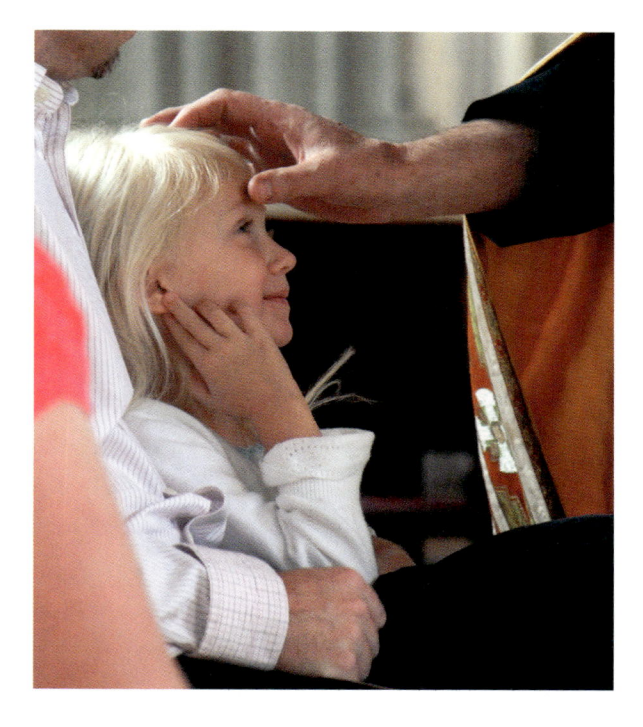

Every year at the Easter Vigil in parishes all over the world people come to be received into the Church. At a time when so many find religion irrelevant, why do these people want to be Catholic? There are as many reasons as there are people.

For example, there were two elderly sisters living around the corner from me a few years ago. Their next-door neighbours were an Englishman and his Swedish wife, Rita, who kept very much to themselves. They had no children and they didn't appear to have any relatives or friends.

After a short illness, the man died and left his devastated wife behind. She asked the two sisters to take her to church with them on the following Sunday morning in her search to make sense of why this had happened. The sisters were very concerned that she would be disappointed, that she would not get what she was looking for by coming along to Mass but they agreed to take her.

After Mass, Rita went to greet the priest, Aidan Galvin. She told him that her husband had just died. She told him that she and her husband were people of no faith; she had come to church that morning to get some answers. She could not recall what the priest had said in his homily but it had touched her deeply and she thanked him. She told him that she wished she belonged to a church like ours so that someone like him could preside at a funeral for her husband, but she thought she wasn't entitled to ask for that. Aidan offered to help though; he prepared a simple and sensitive liturgy for her husband at the local crematorium.

This brief encounter Rita had with Aidan and with her neighbours ended up changing everything for her. She asked if she could join the RCIA group in the parish. The elderly sisters were her godparents and she became a Catholic.

I have to ask you: "Was this all a coincidence or was God's hand guiding it?"

Stages and steps

Sherry Waddell in her book *Forming Intentional Disciples* describes the spiritual process, saying that it moves the thresholds (or stages) in this sequence: trust, curiosity, openness and seeking.

1. **Initial trust**: a person is able to trust or has a positive association with Jesus Christ, the Church or a Christian believer. Rita trusted her neighbours and that was the bridge that moved her towards God.
2. **Spiritual curiosity**: Rita found herself intrigued by Jesus and the Church and she joined the RCIA to find out more.
3. **Spiritual openness**: as she progressed through the RCIA, she was open to the possibility of personal and spiritual change.
4. **Spiritual seeking**: Rita moved to actively seeking to know the God who was calling her. She was seeking to know whether she could commit to Christ in his Church.

Can you see how Rita went through the stages? It's important to note that people don't usually go through these categories neatly or simply as Rita did; they do so in the changing moods and circumstances of their lives. Sometimes, it all takes place in a short period of time and it is possible to observe the transition from beginning to end but, in most cases, we don't see it. My own formation took much longer and it had several gaps!

The encounters I have included in this book are rich in potential and require an awareness and sensitivity on the part of those of us active in Church life to the possibilities inherent within them.

> ### Points for reflection and discussion
> - Have you ever experienced a situation such as Rita's, where one kindness leads to another?
> - Think about a time when you recognised God's hand in an incident like this.
> - This priest seized the opportunity to reach out to Rita – and these two elderly sisters were willing to take her to church even though they doubted. What do you think you would have done?

Opportunities of evangelisation when couples ask to marry in the Church

When a couple come to the church to book a wedding, it may be the first time they are approaching a person in authority they do not know to say they want to be married. They will have told friends and family, people at work, possibly the jeweller. They can relate to all of them without too much difficulty because they have some idea of the assumptions that are being made about them. To book the wedding, however, puts their proposed relationship in a new light – especially if they have preconceived notions about the Church.

In the UK, marriages between two Catholics active in the life of the Church are rare. Marriages between people of different Christian denominations are more usual and a marriage between a Catholic and someone who professes no faith is becoming the norm. The couple may have anxieties about how they will be received if they do not know the priest or if they are non-practising. Chances are that the couple are living together and they may not be sure how the priest will react to this; the Church and their request opens up avenues of evangelisation.

Marriage preparation

For most people, marriage preparation means sending out the invitations, arranging the reception and seating plan, buying the wedding dress, organising outfits for the groom and the rest of the wedding party and parents. It means arranging for flowers and cars and favours.

For couples marrying in Church, however, there is another dimension. The couple is asking to marry in the sight of God, where they will give themselves to each other for better, for worse, for richer or poorer, in sickness and in health, to love and cherish, till death do them part. When one partner is not baptised or is an unbeliever, s/he may be willing to marry in the Church out of respect for their Catholic partner.

In this case, they need to be made aware of the life-long commitment involved in getting married in the Catholic Church.

The Bishops' Conference of England and Wales released its first set of guidelines for marriage preparation in the autumn of 2016. The guidelines were influenced by Pope Francis' exhortation on marriage and family life, *Amoris Laetitia*, which acknowledged the complexity of today's society and the challenges faced by the family. The Pope encouraged a "greater effort on the part of the whole Christian community in preparing those who are about to be married… [and] the synod fathers agreed on the need to involve the entire community more extensively by stressing the witness of families themselves" (*Amoris Laetitia,* 206*)*.

The guidelines tell us that this could be accomplished by introducing the couple to the parish community and for the community to welcome them, pray for them and to assure them of their continuing support as they prepare for their marriage. A simple welcome ritual could be celebrated at the beginning of a Sunday Eucharist in the parish, when the couple might be blessed (including the blessing of the engagement ring).

In addition, the guidelines suggest that married couples run the marriage preparation sessions, and they mentor the engaged couples and pray for engaged couples during their engagement. The parish might also get involved in preparing the church for the wedding itself. Communicating the good news of a wedding taking place in the parish and asking for prayer and continuing support through the parish bulletin, notice boards, social media, and related ways of communication, is recommended – especially because the wedding day is a significant moment of evangelisation.

At the wedding itself, the bride and groom say "I do" to the wedding vows, but the presence of the Church community supports the couple throughout their married life. All those present are acknowledged to be saying to the couple, "We do", we witness and support your marriage.

The core content of marriage preparation recommended in the guidelines include issues such as the promise of commitment the couple will be making to one another, and the importance of open communication and conflict management. Discussing these issues can help the couple to focus on the promise of fidelity they are making to one another. The guidelines also recommend that the couple should discuss their expectations of marriage, the uniqueness of married love (and the power of affirmation, appreciation, giving and receiving forgiveness), what they understand and agree to in terms of how they will nurture their intimacy with one another, family life, having children and the responsibilities involved.

Part of the preparation will also include the planning for the liturgy of the wedding. The celebration of self-giving and personal relationship is now expressed in modern liturgies. When we are planning the liturgy with the couple, we have an ideal opportunity to communicate our belief that the love, concern and self-giving that each has for the other expresses Christ's love for each of them. Human friendship is the most basic sacrament of God's saving presence among us; it reflects and makes credible the reality of God's love for humans. In loving and being loved, each person learns that honest self-appreciation is the psychological grounding for believing the awesome Gospel of God's love for humankind.

God's love is wider than the love expressed in this relationship, yet this moment encapsulates that wideness and divine generosity. Something important is missing from the wedding if this aspect is absent. In preparing the liturgy for the wedding, we can introduce ideas in the choice of the hymns, scripture readings and bidding prayers. Their personal choice will enable them to make the liturgy their own and, done well, offers the priest, pastoral assistant or music minister the opportunity to catechise the couple.

Marriage preparation offers Catholics who have lapsed (or just stopped attending Mass after they were confirmed) a chance to reconnect with the Church – and, when this is the case, it is an opportunity of evangelisation.

We only get the chance of this kind of brief encounter of evangelisation with people when they come to be married in the Church. We probably spend less than ten hours with them – including the liturgy preparation. But, in that brief encounter, we are ministering to profound and life-giving matters.

> **Points for reflection and discussion**
>
> Imagine that you have been asked to prepare a couple for marriage. As they prepare to promise fidelity to one another, what advice would you give:
>
> - On the promise of commitment they will be making?
> - On the need for open communication?
> - On how they will deal with conflict management?
> - On putting God at the heart of their relationship?

Opportunities of evangelisation at funerals

A funeral is quite unlike a baptism or a wedding. There are no parents seeking something for their child; there is no couple looking for something for themselves. The context is different. Something has already happened; someone has died and the family are doing their best to cope with it.

The approach to a priest or a pastoral assistant will come from the family if they (or the deceased person) are involved in the Church. It may come from the undertaker otherwise. Whatever the circumstances, a bereavement is what brings many people to the Church. They may want to celebrate the life of the deceased. They may be struggling to understand the meaning of suffering and death. There will be a mixture of practising and non-practising Catholics and there will be people of other faiths or none who knew the deceased; but, no matter how disconnected from the Church and from religion these people are, grief is an evangelisation opportunity.

The kind of welcome, support and kindness the bereaved family experience when they approach the Church often brings people back to the parish for support in the future – especially if what they experience is different from the experiences and notions that led them to leave Church in the first place.

No matter how connected or disconnected people are from the Church and religion, grief can offer opportunities of evangelisation for the family and friends of the deceased. We know, for example, belief in the afterlife has diminished in the world we live in.

I had a workman in my house recently and he noticed my Christian artefacts. He told me that he is an unbeliever and said that he envies people who believe. He'd love to know that he will see his wife again so that he could tell her how much he had loved her. He didn't think he had told her often enough when she was still here. He grew up in an orphanage and he said he wasn't good at expressing his feelings (although he was doing pretty well expressing them to me!).

He asked me if I really believe in the afterlife and, of course, I said I do. Believing in the message of eternal life gives me the hope of seeing my loved ones again and that gives me comfort. I told him that I was sure his wife knew how much he had loved her and that I would pray that God would give him the gift of hope that he will see her again.

Bereavement teams

Lay people often find opportunities of evangelisation such as this nowadays when they find themselves in a conversation with someone at work or with a neighbour who is searching to understand the meaning of suffering and death.

Another avenue for evangelisation available to lay people is through bereavement support teams who offer practical support, contact information for professional agencies that might be needed, a chat, or a chance to meet for coffee. They offer to help with form-filling, and in some cases, where the deceased was the one bringing the bereaved to Mass, offer them a lift so that they can get to Mass or to events in the parish.

Is the Mass always most appropriate for a funeral?

That brings us to echo the following question posed by Bernard Cotter (*The Tablet*, 9 November 2013): "Is a full funeral Mass always the appropriate way for the Church to mark the passing of one of its members – particularly for someone who rarely was part of such an assembly for a long number of years?" Bernard Cotter is a parish priest in Cork, Ireland. He says that the baptised and confirmed Catholic may be entitled to a funeral Mass at the end of life, but is this always the most suitable, or pastorally appropriate, celebration?

Bernard says that, if a funeral liturgy other than a funeral Mass were offered, it should be possible to include within the structure some of the elements desired by those who learn what funerals are from cultural sources other than Church involvement because the funeral liturgy is not a Mass. For example, if there is no presentation of gifts of bread and wine for the Eucharist, a bringing up or placing of mementos can become a natural prelude to the ceremony, rather than a pre-Mass duplication of what ought to happen during the liturgy.

In fact, the Church offers various opportunities for personal choices in each of the three stages of the funeral (prayer vigil, funeral liturgy, committal). Secular poems and songs often fit best in the prayer vigil, but there is also an opportunity for "Words in Remembrance" towards the end of the funeral liturgy in both Eucharistic and non-Eucharistic liturgies. However, care should be taken that the words of any material is in keeping with our Christian faith. Engaging the family of the deceased non-involved parishioner will also serve as an outreach to the unchurched.

Bernard says that to continue to insist that the funeral Mass is the only suitable liturgy to mark the passing of a Catholic led by a priest would be to limit the Church's engagement with those seeking solace at a traumatic time in life. The taking of a more flexible approach by offering a non-Eucharistic liturgy led by a lay person might open up the Church's riches to a whole generation little exposed to them. By reaching out to meet the needs of the grieving friends and family, they may see the Church from an entirely new perspective and that could lead to the spiritual curiosity Sherry Waddell talks about.

The planning of such a non-Eucharistic liturgy might also provide a local pastor with a forum for sharing his own faith about the afterlife because of Christ's death and resurrection, and might indeed lead to an opening for Christian motifs that the war over the inclusion or non-inclusion of a eulogy would make impossible.

The seemingly easier approach is to concentrate on the funeral Mass and seek to adapt it to the needs presented by mourners today, needs that are heavily influenced by sources other than the Church itself. The braver and more sustaining course of action in the long-term might be for pastors to recognise that all who seek funeral liturgies are not at the same level of faith and practice, and to tailor the liturgies on offer to those who seek them.

Lay-led funerals

Although lay ministers already lead funerals in some parts of the world where no priest or deacon is available, in 2012 the Archdiocese of Liverpool was the first diocese in England and Wales to commission lay people to lead funerals. The decision by Archbishop Patrick Kelly represented the first time such a step was authorised by the Catholic Church in England and Wales.

Maureen Knight, who is responsible for pastoral care at Liverpool Archdiocese, says the scheme has been a great success in Liverpool. In a recent article in *Catholic Truth* (16 November 2016), she said that they've had 120 people go through the training programme there and the negativity around it has been minimal.

They find that people who are not used to being at Mass and don't know the prayers of the Mass or how to respond to the priest are more comfortable with the non-Eucharistic funeral. Another benefit of making this change to lay leaders has helped make the "care of the bereaved to become the responsibility of the whole community." The lay funeral minister can "be with the family beforehand, talk about things they might be afraid to talk to a priest about," she said. In addition, they are likely to have more time available to visit the bereaved afterwards than the priest does, to look after them a bit more.

In the 1997 Vatican document on the laity fulfilling priestly duties, *Instruction on certain questions regarding the collaboration of the non-ordained faithful in the sacred ministry of the priest*, it says:

> the non-ordained faithful may lead the ecclesiastical obsequies provided that there is a true absence of sacred ministers and that they adhere to the prescribed liturgical norms.

It also states:

> In the present circumstances of growing de-Christianisation and of abandonment of religious

practice, death and the time of obsequies can be one of the most opportune pastoral moments in which the ordained minister can meet with the non-practising members of the faithful… [so] it is thus desirable that priests and deacons, even at some sacrifice to themselves, should preside personally at funeral rites in accordance with local custom, so as to pray for the dead and be close to their families, thus availing of an opportunity for appropriate evangelization.

In many places in Africa, lay leaders carry out funeral services without a priest for two reasons. Firstly, it means that the bodies can be buried soon after death; and secondly, parishes cover vast areas and it may not be possible to arrange for a priest to come to the funeral immediately after a death. The priest then comes a month or so later to celebrate Mass with the community when people have had the time to organise his visit. I wonder if this idea might offer a happy compromise.

Points for reflection and discussion

- Reflect on/discuss this statement: "We must meet people where they are – and not where we would like them to be."
- Reflect on/discuss your views on a lay-led funeral.
- How about the idea of a non-Eucharistic liturgy instead of a liturgy?

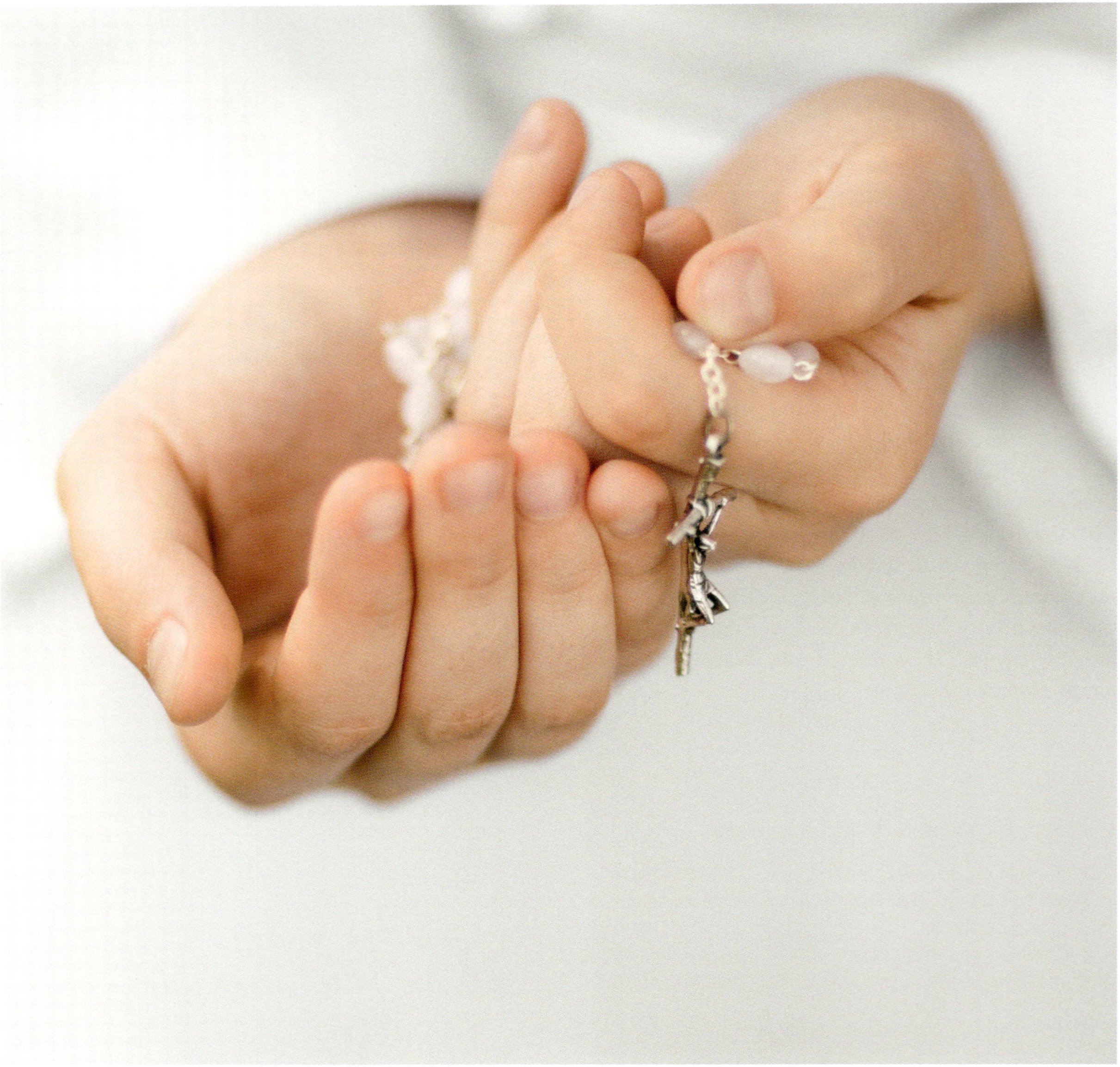

CHAPTER SIX

BRIEF ENCOUNTERS OF EVANGELISATION IN OUR PARISH CATECHETICAL PROGRAMMES

Catechesis as a work of evangelisation

The *General Directory for Catechesis* tells us that

> The aim of catechesis is to put people not only in touch, but also in communion and intimacy, with Jesus Christ. (GDC 80)

> Catholics who come to know Jesus Christ have always sought ways of explaining their experience of him to others and of manifesting this experience through faith-directed action. In understanding the tasks of catechesis, we turn, of course to Christ, who revealed to his disciples the secrets of the reign of God. (GDC 84-85)

The GDC also tells us that

> The reflections of the General Assembly of the Synod of Bishops of October 1974 on the theme of Evangelization in the Contemporary World constitute a decisive milestone for catechesis. The propositions subsequently drawn up by the Synod were presented to Pope Paul VI, who promulgated the post-synodal Apostolic Exhortation *Evangelii Nuntiandi* of 8 December 1975. This document enunciates, amongst other things, a particularly important principle, namely, that of catechesis as a work of evangelization in the context of the mission of the Church. (GDC 4)

Our parish catechetical programmes offer us many privileged opportunities of evangelisation through our encounters with adults and children. Parents will attend sessions during their children's preparation for First Holy Communion and confirmation, and these sessions offer an opportunity for adult faith formation. This may be their first experience of evangelisation since they were confirmed as children.

First Holy Communion preparation

As I've already mentioned, I had been away from the Church for a long time and my son, Nicholas, was baptised during a visit to the USA. When we returned to England, he was about three-and-a-half years old and I thought he needed the kind of stimulation he would get at pre-school. He was offered a place at a local Montessori school run by the Franciscan Sisters of Mill Hill, where I thought he'd learn all he needed to know about being Catholic – so I was off the hook.

Children are evangelisers

Nicholas stayed on at the Montessori school after pre-school; and, when he began Year 3, his teacher asked how many children in the class wanted to prepare for their First Holy Communion that year. Nicholas came home and told me that he wanted to do it. The school as a community attended Mass in the parish each Friday morning and he liked going to church. He told me that the teacher said we would have to start going to Mass on Sundays. I told him that once a week was enough, but he said, "Mrs Wilkinson says we have to go to Mass on Sundays."

It was not easy for me to come back to the Church after twenty years but it was made easier by a lovely priest, Noel Travers, who was also chaplain at Nicholas' school. My mother was delighted. She came for the First Holy Communion celebration along with my godmother and a couple of cousins. But, in the summertime after Nicholas' First Communion, we went on holiday to France and didn't go to Mass on the Sundays while we were there so I thought I was again excluded. In addition, Noel left the parish for a new ministry and so I ended up drifting away again and Nicholas went back to going to Mass only on Friday mornings.

Reflecting back now, I can see that although I had returned to the "practice" of the faith temporarily, I had not had an encounter with Jesus. I knew a little about him and I'd learned through Nicholas' preparation programme a certain amount about the post-Vatican II teachings of the Church, but I had not gained a personal familiarity with Jesus – and so, it didn't "take".

"Sacramental preparation for the children can also help the community reveal and celebrate the true presence of Jesus in our midst"

Practising parents and parents who are practising

I don't know if it is true, but thirty years ago I had the impression that I was the only parent in Nicholas' class who was not practising my faith. I felt very much an outsider. That demographic has changed enormously and, as I understand it, many parents of the children preparing for First Holy Communion do not attend Mass regularly. In some parishes, they ask the children to "sign in" with the priest or a catechist to prove that they have been to Mass each week as a condition of the programme.

In some ways, I am scandalised by this practice because I have come to believe that God invites us; he never forces us and I am afraid we are giving the wrong message to these parents and children by making this demand on them. On the other hand, the Eucharist – indeed, the whole of our faith – will only make sense to a child in the context of his or her own family *and* community, for it is in these relationships that the children will experience first-hand the poor, the sick, the lonely, the suffering – all those Jesus came to serve and to save.

Parents (even if they are not practising) want what's best for their children. Many parents who were brought up Catholic want for their children the religious experience they had when they had when they received their First Communion. However, if the children don't experience being part of the Eucharistic community, how will they be able to experience their First Holy Communion as an important and exciting day in their religious life?

The children are prepared for their First Communion through the efforts of three groups of people: each child's own family, the catechists and the parish community as a whole. The members of these groups in the faith community, each with special experiences of what the Eucharist means to them, come together to pass on their faith and the Church's tradition on the Eucharist to the children in the parish.

We will now look at how the children and their parents are prepared. Then we will look at ways we can use this sacramental preparation as a **moment of evangelisation** for the community as a whole.

First Holy Communion preparation for the parents and the children

It is important that parents be involved in preparing the children for their First Communion. Many of them will have few if any other opportunities for adult catechesis. If they are going to support their children as they prepare for their First Communion, it is crucial that they know about and understand what the children are learning.

In many parishes today, there are parents' meetings during the course of the programme. In some parishes, the parents meet in one room and the children meet in another room at the same time – each of them learning about one of the themes in the programme, each at their own level of understanding. This has been the way things worked for the last twenty or thirty years or so. But a new approach, "family catechesis", is now being introduced. One programme in particular has caught my attention: *Growing Up Catholic*. It involves the parents as catechists of their own children. In times past, parents often **believed that it was the job of the parish or the school** to teach their child about religion. But today we know that if a child has any chance at all of growing up with faith, it's because of their parents.

The method used in *Growing Up Catholic* is that, instead of teaching the children and/or giving talks to the parents, the catechists evangelise the parents so that they can catechise **their own children**. This focus is important because we know that if the parents are not invested at a high enough level to walk their own children through the formation and preparation process, there's virtually nothing you can do to substitute that. Evangelisation is a life-long process. Practising parents can benefit as they grow in faith and in their commitment to be followers of Christ. Non-practising (or non-Catholic) parents will benefit and may come back to (or join) the Church. The biggest benefit is for the children since there is nothing that can substitute for parents showing interest and sharing their faith with their children.

This programme can be adapted by the parents of children who have learning disabilities, which means that these children and their parents can join in the community sessions. I see this as an important bonus to the programme because not all parish priests, catechists and parents understand the value of including learning-disabled children in their programmes and consequently, sometimes, exclude them from being prepared for their First Holy Communion altogether.

People with special needs can mediate the Good News

Aidan Galvin once told a touching story about a new parish priest who asked a mother why her teenage son with Down's syndrome was not receiving Communion each Sunday but was instead coming up for a blessing. She had been told that since her son would not understand, he could not receive. The priest tried to prepare the boy, but was not sure how much the boy understood.

Nevertheless, he determined that the boy should make his First Communion. When the time came, the priest asked the congregation to allow the boy and his mother to receive Communion first. He gave the boy the host; the boy turned, he broke the host in half and gave half to his mother.

Think about it. We sometimes imagine that we are giving something to people with learning disabilities who are perceived as lacking something; and we end by realising that they have enriched us. Finding ways to mediate the Good News of the Gospel to people with special needs has led to the development of alternative methods of catechesis which do not rely solely on the written or verbal.

People of all abilities can benefit from these approaches which are heart-centred, not head-centred. The *General Directory of Catechesis* tells us that "growth in our understanding of disability, along with progress in specialised pedagogy, makes it possible and desirable for *all* to have adequate catechesis" (GDC 189). Disability advisers are developing multi-sensory approaches and priests, catechists and parents are being encouraged to use music, song, movement, symbols and sign language to help adults and children with special needs prepare for and celebrate the sacraments.

Parents still face obstacles

Sadly, however, some parents still face obstacles when their children want to prepare for First Communion with their friends of the same age. They are told that their child might disturb the others in the group or that their child will not be able to understand the preparation well enough. Parishes might think of ways to help these families. For example, they might arrange for them to have a regular place to sit, or they might provide a good children's liturgy to reduce the time the child is in the church. This would also serve to provide a Liturgy of the Word with activities at a level the children can understand.

Parents might find that their children are less fidgety if they have something in their hands such as rosary beads or a book with symbols and activities when they go to Mass.

Our parishes must be places of welcome for all of us. Our baptism means that each of us belongs fully to God's wider family of the Church and we share a responsibility to love, to care and to serve one another – to make that belonging real.

The community shares in the First Holy Communion preparation too

First Communion is an important event in the life of the whole Eucharistic community. Since the children are being prepared to be further initiated into the local parish, the parish needs to be aware of, and be involved in, the children's preparation. Sacramental preparation for the children can also help the community reveal and celebrate the true presence of Jesus in our midst.

In many parishes, there are special Masses as part of the programme. The children help to animate Mass on Sundays focused on the themes in the Mass: gathering, listening to the word, giving thanks and praise, taking and eating and being sent out to bring Christ to those we meet. These masses can help regularly practising Catholics deepen their understanding of the Mass and the different ways Christ is always present in his Church:

- **As we gather:** We gather believing that Christ is present because he said that "where two or three are gathered, I am present" (Matthew 18:20).
- **In the word:** "When Sacred Scriptures are read in Church, God himself speaks to his people, and Christ, present in his word, proclaims the Gospel" (*General Instruction of the Roman Missal* (GIRM), 29).
- **In the Eucharist:** "Christ is truly, really and substantially present" (Catholic Bishops' Conference of England and Wales, *One Bread One Body*, 50).
- **And, in the priest who presides at the Mass:** "By his bearing and by the way he [the priest] pronounces the divine words he must convey the living presence of Christ" (GIRM, 93).

(*See* also Second Vatican Council, *Sacrosanctum Concilium* (Constitution on the Sacred Liturgy), SC 7.)

These celebrations make visible the children who are preparing for the special time when they will receive Jesus in the Eucharist for the first time; and the parish community can be invited to reflect on the gift they are given each time they receive Communion. They can also pray for the children and their families during this time of preparation.

Confirmation preparation

The sacrament of confirmation provides us with a real opportunity to re-evangelise young adults in the Church. But preparation for this sacrament isn't only about getting ready for the rite. It's about getting ready for a lifetime of faith; it's about recognising that we are a Eucharistic people and what that entails.

There is no specific age at which confirmation can be conferred, once the age of reason has been reached (*see* Canon 891). Pastorally, there are different views as to which is the best age. The readiness of the person to receive the sacrament is ultimately more important than the age, and any preparation needs to be adapted to the age and maturity of the candidate. It is for each diocese to decide upon their policy regarding the age of confirmation and how people are prepared.

Confusion about the age and the purpose of confirmation

When he was thirteen, Nicholas wrote the parish priest a compelling letter asking to join the confirmation programme. The priest had asked young people who would be fourteen by the following summer to write to him if they wanted to join the confirmation programme, explaining why they wished to be confirmed. Nicholas' letter explained that he was ready to confirm publicly that he was a Catholic, that he hoped this would qualify him to join the programme – and that he had Jewish friends who were thirteen and were celebrating their bar mitzvah (the "rite of passage" in Judaism from childhood to adulthood). He suspected Jesus had been bar mitzvah'd at thirteen too – and he wondered why Catholics had to wait until they were fourteen to be confirmed. The catechist replied that Nicholas was not mature enough at thirteen years of age.

Shortly after that, we met a woman and her nine-year-old son who were preparing to become Catholic. She was attending the RCIA (Rite of Christian Initiation for Adults) and the boy was attending the parish RE programme. At the Easter Vigil a few months later, they were baptised, confirmed and received the Eucharist. Nicholas wanted to know why this boy could be confirmed at nine years of age when he had been told that he was not mature enough at thirteen years of age.

> *"Unless the confirmation programme engages the young people, their engagement in the parish will not continue after the celebration of their confirmation"*

The parish priest explained that all three sacraments make up the process of belonging to the Church (called Christian Initiation) for unbaptised adults through the RCIA. Part II of the Rite, the Christian Initiation of Children of Catechetical Age (CICCA), tells us that this is also the way unbaptised children between the ages of seven and fourteen celebrate the Sacraments of Initiation.

He said, in fact, that the Eastern liturgical practice is to celebrate all three Sacraments of Initiation, even with infants. All of that might have made sense to him; but I was left wondering what the sacrament of confirmation was for and no doubt others are puzzled too, when their diocese announces that in future local Catholic children will be confirmed before their First Communion, while other dioceses will stick with Communion first.

Whether we confirm children or teenagers, it is important for them to be offered the kind of catechesis which paves the way for an ongoing personal commitment – and not just a commitment that's definitively made on the day they are confirmed, a commitment that experience shows can subsequently fail in practice. Catechesis should remind us all that we are invited to say "Yes" and to renew our commitment to Christ each and every time we receive the Eucharist. The Eucharist is the one repeatable sacrament of initiation – the sacrament of commitment and recommitment.

What the Church can learn from the young

An editorial in *The Tablet* (19 January 2017) talked about young people as practising idealists when "authenticity is at a premium and the world is a mess". Pope Francis has decided that his next project is to understand the young and where the generation dubbed the "millennials" are coming from. He wants to harness their hopes and ideals for the common good, so that they will join him in undoing that mess.

Accordingly, in 2018 the theme for the 50th General Assembly of the Synod of Bishops, "Young People, the Faith and the Discernment of Vocation", was announced on 6 October 2016. A Catholic News Agency report in January 2017 says that, in choosing this specific theme, the Church not only wants to ask herself "how she can lead young people to recognise and accept the call to the fullness of life and love" but also "to ask young people to help her in identifying the most effective ways to announce the Good News today".

Pope Francis recalled how when he was in Krakow for World Youth Day over the summer (2016), he had asked the youth on several occasions, "Can we change things?" to which they responded with a loud, resounding "Yes!" "That shout came from your young and youthful hearts, which do not tolerate injustice and cannot bow to a throw-away culture nor give in to the globalisation of indifference," Francis said, urging young people to "listen to the cry arising from your inner selves!"

"A better world can be built also as a result of your efforts, your desire to change and your generosity," he said, telling them not to be afraid of the "bold choices" proposed to them by the Holy Spirit and to not delay "when your conscience asks you to take risks in following the Master." Pope Francis said that "The Church also wishes to listen to your voice, your sensitivities and your faith; even your doubts and your criticism," adding that youth should not be shy in making their voices heard, even to their priests.

Pointing to the example of how St Benedict urged his abbots "to consult, even the young, before any important decision" since "the Lord often reveals to the younger what is best", Francis said that this is also the case for the upcoming synod. In order to prepare for the synod, the bishops of England and Wales have released a survey, which will help inform a report that will be sent to the Vatican before the synod, which is scheduled for October 2018. The "Youth Poll on Life, Faith and Vocational Discernment" invites answers from those between the ages of thirteen and twenty-nine years of age of all religions and none.

> ### Points for reflection and discussion
>
> Consider how you would reply to young Catholics who want answers to these questions:
>
> - "Why have a rulebook?"
> - "What is the sacrament of confirmation and why should I be confirmed?

Confirmation programmes for teenagers

Confirmation programmes must engage the young people and help them to see the Church's teaching is relevant to them. I have a fair bit of experience as a confirmation catechist and I find that a programme that offers (and trusts) teenagers to explore Church teaching works. The method is inspired by the story of the Walk to Emmaus. Let me share what happened in a session on the Ten Commandments:

- Just as Jesus joined the disciples and discussed what was happening in their lives, we begin the session by telling a "real life" story. In the session on the Ten Commandments, I like to share how my first instinct is to say "no" when I am told to do something. I show the candidates a cartoon of Moses coming down from Mount Sinai with the commandments. Two men at the base of the mountain are saying to one another, "Don't you think it would be better to call them recommendations?" The candidates are then invited to share their response to my story. That leads nicely into the second stage.
- Just as Jesus opened the scriptures, we read the scripture of Moses presenting the Ten Commandments (Exodus 20). Then, one by one, we look at each of the commandments and give a little input and/or ask questions. In small groups, the candidates are invited to discuss the issues. The role of the catechist is to enable conversation, allowing the candidates to reflect on the Church's teaching.
- When we got to the fifth commandment: "Thou

Chapter Six: Brief encounters of evangelisation in our parish catechetical programmes

shall not kill", they said you can't go around killing each other. I said that I doubted that any of them had killed another human being; but I asked what they thought the Church's teaching might be on how we should respect life. For example, what is our obligation is to ourselves and to the planet in regards respect for life? It was very heartening to hear the views of these young idealists, who explained that they didn't think it is wrong to chop down trees so long as young trees are planted to replace them. On the other hand, they said it is a lack of respect for life to kill a coral reef since it takes an extremely long time to replace and once again serve its important purpose within the process of organic life on earth. And, when it comes to respecting human life, they said it is the job of the family, the school and the government to protect the most vulnerable members, namely, the children, those who are weak or ill and those who are elderly and need to be cared for.

- The disciples' eyes were opened and they recognised Jesus at the breaking of the bread. In this session, I was very encouraged to hear how strongly these young people held to their principles. They were surprised to discover that the Church's teaching is in line with their views on ecological issues.

I'd like to share one more story about a session based on the Creed. The young people are invited to reflect on what they mean when they say "I believe in…" After each statement, a short story is told to stimulate their discussion. For "I believe in Jesus Christ", I told a story written by Gerard W. Hughes in his book, *Oh God, Why?* He asks us to imagine that there is a ring at our doorbell one evening; and, when we open the door, we discover that the visit is Jesus, the Risen Lord himself. We believe him but don't know what to say. You can't shut the door on him; you can't tell him to go away and come back on Sunday. No, you call everyone in the house and tell Jesus to make himself at home, to stay as long as he likes. Then, Hughes invites us to take a fortnight's leap in our imagination.

> Jesus has accepted your invitation and he is still with you. How are things at home now? You remember that disturbing passage in the Gospel where Jesus says, "I have come not to bring peace, but the sword, to set daughter against mother, daughter-in-law against mother-in-law, son against father." The letter to the Hebrews says "Jesus Christ is the same today as he was yesterday and as he will be forever", so presumably there has been a bit of friction over family meals in the last two weeks, some members leaving the table, slamming doors, possibly the front door, never to return. You invited Jesus to make himself at home, so he has begun inviting his friends to your house. You remember what people said of his friends in the Gospel, how he dined with sinners. What kind of people do you see coming now to your house, what are the neighbours saying, and what is happening to the local property values? Then you decide that you must not keep Jesus all to yourself, so you

arrange for him to give a talk at the local church. You remember that scene in the Gospel where he addresses the scribes, Pharisees and chief priests and assures them that the criminals and the prostitutes will get into the kingdom of God before they do. He gives the same message to a gathering of men and women at St Jude's parish and there is uproar, the parish losing its principal benefactors.

You return home with Jesus, your Saviour, who has now become your problem. What are you to do? You cannot throw out the Lord of all creation. So you look around the house, find a suitable cupboard, clear it out, decorate it, sparing no expense, get a good strong lock on it and put Jesus inside. Outside you can have a lamp and flowers, and each time you pass, bow reverently, so that you now have Jesus and he does not interfere anymore! (*Oh God, Why?* (Oxford: The Bible Reading Fellowship, 1993), 23-24)

Naturally, I changed St Jude's Parish to our parish name. I thought I read the story well with lots of feeling and I invited the candidates to discuss it and to share with one another what they mean when they say "I believe in Jesus Christ". There was a very long silence, followed by very quiet conversation between the candidates. I wasn't sure what to think.

The next day, I met one of the candidate's mothers, who asked me what I had done to the kids during that session. Her son returned home and talked with them for hours about the story. He challenged them about their image of Jesus; he challenged them about what it meant to them to practise what Jesus taught – and he asked them if they would invite Jesus to come and make himself at home in their house.

I have many stories like this I can tell; these encounters with the young people were very powerful moments of evangelisation.

Preparing for the sacrament of reconciliation

All the sacraments are gifts for the life of the Church and, as we mature, we must be prepared to question and develop our own understanding of them. This is particularly true of the sacrament of reconciliation, which reminds us of the first and most important element of God's love for us and the expression of that love through forgiveness and encouragement.

In his excellent book on this subject, *The Quality of Mercy*, Bishop John Arnold writes that when God forgives, his forgiveness is complete and perfect; it is as if our faults and sins of the past never occurred. When we come to the sacrament and ask for forgiveness of our God, who is perfect love, then we must believe that the forgiveness that we receive is not the human sort of forgiveness that so often hangs on to the offences of the past.

According to Bishop John, the sacrament of reconciliation offers an opportunity, first and foremost, to introduce the fact of God's love. Do the penitents know that God loves them, just as they are? Do they know that God has always loved them – even loved them into being – and that, as St Paul says, nothing can ever separate them from the love of Christ? These are the theological foundations of this sacrament.

Preparing the penitent to celebrate the sacrament of reconciliation

Bishop John offers some thoughts on the practice of the examination of conscience. There is no single method; we need to discover the way that works for us.

With the first method, there are three things to bear in mind:

1. The examination is not something we use only to prepare for the sacrament of reconciliation. It can be used to ask for forgiveness any time we ask for it. It can help to celebrate the Penitential Act at the beginning of Mass. And, it should always be part of our preparation for the celebration of the sacrament of reconciliation.
2. Whenever we begin to scrutinise what we are and what we may have done, we may be disappointed by what we see. Our efforts to come closer to God may well reveal that we are further from the holiness we seek than we thought. Underlying our discovery and our discomfort is the certain truth that God loves us as we are – even though we may feel less good about ourselves. And, when we are reflecting on our lives and discovering things about ourselves, we are on the way forward and we can be assured that is most pleasing to God.
3. The examination of conscience should not just dwell on what has gone wrong, but should be a reflection on what has been good – things I have done well and an appreciation of what I have received.

In the second method of examination, a passage of scripture is taken and the simple question is asked, "Have I lived this today?" He offers an example which concerns behaviour that we can adapt for our lives, St Paul's great hymn to love in his First Letter to the Corinthians (13:1-13):

> If I speak in the tongues of mortals and of angels, but do not have love, I am a noisy gong or a clanging cymbal. And if I have prophetic powers, and understand all mysteries and all knowledge, and if I have all faith, so as to remove mountains, but do not have love, I am nothing. If I give away all my possessions, and if I hand over my body so that I may boast, but do not have love, I gain nothing.
>
> Love is patient; love is kind; love is not envious or boastful or arrogant or rude. It does not insist on its own way; it is not irritable or resentful; it does not rejoice in wrongdoing, but rejoices in the truth. It bears all things, believes all things, hopes all things, endures all things.

Love never ends. But as for prophecies, they will come to an end; as for tongues, they will cease; as for knowledge, it will come to an end. For we know only in part, and we prophesy only in part; but when the complete comes, the partial will come to an end. When I was a child, I spoke like a child, I thought like a child, I reasoned like a child; when I became an adult, I put an end to childish ways. For now we see in a mirror, dimly, but then we will see face to face. Now I know only in part; then I will know fully, even as I have been fully known. And now faith, hope, and love abide, these three; and the greatest of these is love.

If we are regular in examining our conscience, Bishop John says we will never be lost for material that we want to bring with us to the sacrament and we will discover priorities for our concern and where it is that we need to be forgiven (*The Quality of Mercy* (London: St Pauls, 1999), 62, 81-83).

Preparing the priest to be a good confessor

At an address in Rome on 17 March 2017, Pope Francis talked to priests about being "good confessors". He said that the confessional is a true and proper place of evangelisation. In fact, there is no more genuine evangelisation than in the encounter with the God of mercy, with the God who is mercy. And, to encounter mercy means to encounter the true face of God, as the Lord Jesus has revealed it. I have a couple of stories (from anonymous sources that I've heard over the years) that put flesh on this.

A man went to confession one Saturday morning and confessed that he had committed adultery. It was the first time he'd ever done anything like that and he was really ashamed. The priest asked him to say three Hail Marys for his penance. The following Saturday, he went back to the same confessional and told the priest that maybe he hadn't heard him properly. He had committed adultery! The priest gave him a decade of the rosary this time. Once again, the following Saturday, he went back to the priest and asked him if he didn't realise how serious his sin was. The priest told him to say all five decades of all four sets of mysteries of the rosary. The man was surprised that the penance had increased so much. The priest assured him that God loves him and that he has always loved him – even in this dark moment when he has disappointed and shocked himself by what he had done. The penance, the priest explained, was not for committing adultery. It was for failing to believe in the mercy of God and failing to accept his forgiveness.

My second story is about a priest and an Irishman arriving at the gates of heaven at the same time. St Peter tells them that they have to have earned ten points while they were on earth in order to get in. The priest says he will go first since he was a priest for fifty years; he said the Divine Office and he said Mass every day. St Peter responded: "One point." The priest said that he visited the sick in his parish regularly. "One more point," said St Peter. The priest wondered if he would ever get to ten. While he was deliberating about what he should say next, St Peter told the Irishman it was his turn to list the ten points he had earned. "Well," he said, "I knew I was weak and that I was tempted to sin; but I also knew I had to rely on the mercy of God to save me." St Peter replied, "Ten points! Come in."

Pope Francis sent a message to bishops, priests and Church workers attending Italy's annual week of liturgical studies on the subject of the sacrament of reconciliation saying that "God's mercy is poured out upon the repentant so that they can change and grow" (Catholic News Service, "Encounter God's mercy in Confession", 23 August 2016). Catholics must be helped to see that when they are forgiven, they must learn to forgive others, the Pope's message continued. The world needs "witnesses of mercy in every sphere", people who can help others desire and learn how to forgive.

Religious education for children not attending Catholic schools

Parish primary schools cannot always accommodate all the applicants they have. In addition, some parents choose to send their children to private schools; and, as more and more parents are both working full-time, they sometimes opt to send their children to schools closer to their workplace. In this case, they rarely manage to get their children into the Catholic schools there because they are outside their parish. When this happens, parishes need to provide religious education for those children.

I Call You Friends is a programme produced by Living and Sharing Our Faith, the National Project of Catechesis and Religious Education of the Catholic Bishops' Conference of England and Wales. The programme follows the liturgical year with three key themes each year: the Church, the sacraments and Christian living. Each of the three terms (autumn, spring and summer) lead up to one of the Church's major celebrations: Christmas, Easter and Pentecost.

These programmes bring a huge range of benefits to the parish. For a start, they provide a "safe" place to welcome people back to the Church who have drifted away. The parents often ask if they can accompany their children to the sessions when they first come to us, only to find that their children's interest fires their own enthusiasm; and, in their own time, they return to the Church with a whole new sense of commitment.

The programme sometimes becomes a recruiting ground for new catechists. The parents begin by helping the children with their drawings and making tea and drinks; they may eventually then lead a small group session and, after their spiritual curiosity has been nurtured, they may agree to attend some catechetical training sessions.

I was leading one of these RE sessions for the children in a parish who were not attending Catholic schools, which was called *Walk with Me* (the predecessor of *I Call You Friends*). One of the non-Catholic mothers asked if she could remain with her two children. I think she was afraid the children were going to be indoctrinated in her husband's faith and she was not

Chapter Six: Brief encounters of evangelisation in our parish catechetical programmes

ENCOUNTERS OF EVANGELISATION 75

altogether comfortable about it – especially given her preconceived notions of Catholicism.

One day, we were scheduled to do a session on prayer and it was a hot day. I asked our helpers to go next door to the newsagent's to buy sufficient ice creams – enough to give each child one. We all thanked God for the gift of the ice cream and asked God to bless it and to bless us, and the children began to eat their treat. As they did, I said God had made the ice cream and I asked them if they wanted to know how he did that.

Ice cream, I said, begins with grass. The farmer plants the seeds in good earth. God plans rain showers and the sun's warming rays to help the seeds grow. The farmer then brings the cows who eat the grass and the cows give us milk; the milk is made into cream and sent to the factory. Sugar cane stalks grow by the grace of God and they also go to the factory, where they get made into sugar which they add to the cream. Then the factory takes fruit and adds it to the cream and sugar creating lots of different flavours of ice cream. They put the ice cream into containers and send them off to the shops where we can buy it. The children interjected "Thank God for ice cream!" after some of my pauses and they all shouted it when they had finished their ice cream and I'd finished my story.

The children were then asked to write a thank you letter to God for something. The youngest child wasn't writing yet so her mum was her scribe. When she finished, the mother asked the child how she would post the letter to God. The child (who was, I guess, four or five) said, "Don't be silly! I don't have to send it to God. He already knows what the letter says. He was here all the while watching you write it for me."

The mother's perception of Catholicism completely changed, and she went on to become a Catholic the following year. Working alongside our little group, *walking with us*, as it were, had produced a fire in her heart and she came to recognise Christ among us and present in the Church.

Points for reflection and discussion

- How would you describe the ideal catechist for these RE programmes for children who are not in Catholic schools?
- If your parish doesn't have such an RE programme, how would you go about setting one up?
- If you were going to write a thank you letter to God today, what would you say to him?

Chapter Six: Brief encounters of evangelisation in our parish catechetical programmes

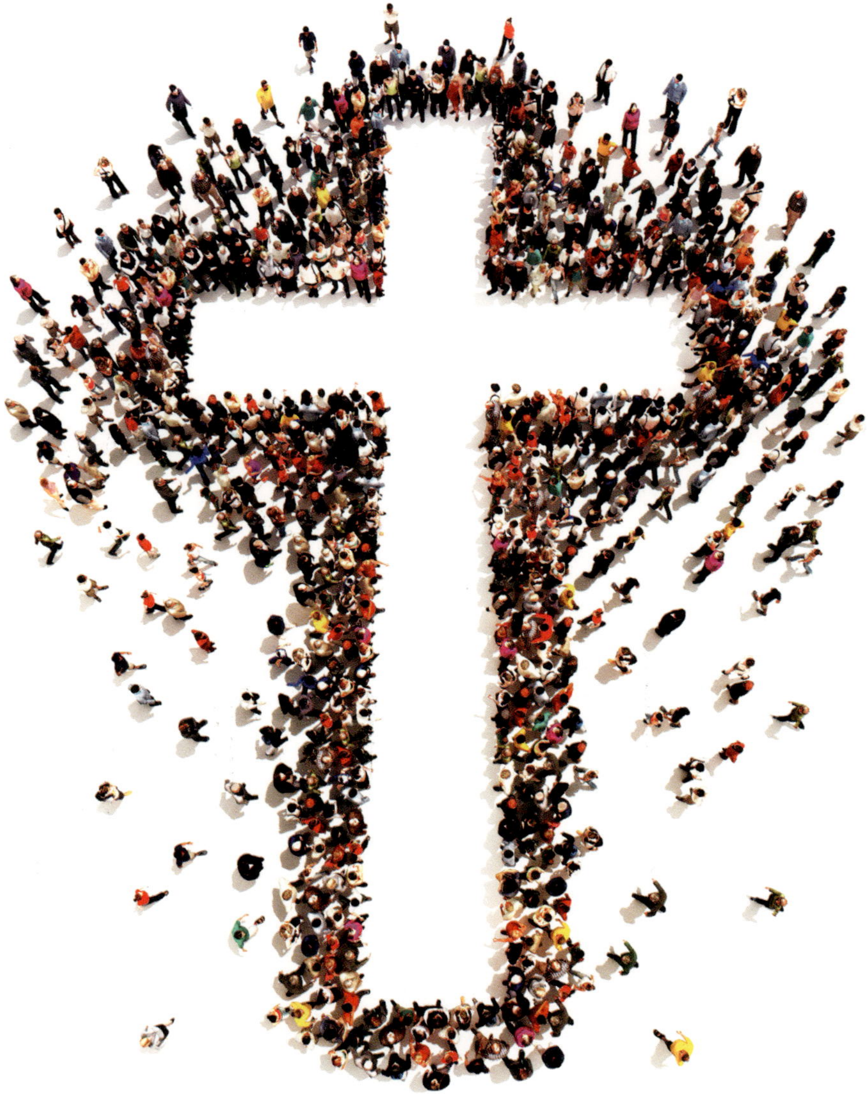

CHAPTER SEVEN

REACHING OUT TO NON-CHURCHGOING CATHOLICS

I've talked about how I drifted away from the Church, returned briefly when Nicholas was receiving his First Holy Communion, but then drifted away again.

When I first came to England from New York, I shared a flat with a Jewish woman called Angela. Neither of us was practising our religion at the time. After a few years, I got married and Angela went to Sweden for her work and she fell in love and wanted to marry Per, a Swedish man, who was willing to convert to Orthodox Judaism since Angela wanted to bring her children up just as she had been raised.

Per embraced Judaism but the Jewish community in Stockholm was small. After their two children were born, they wanted to be part of an active community with young families so they moved to England, even though this meant lowering the standard of living they had in Sweden.

I was delighted that Angela was back and even more delighted that they bought a house in the next road. Nicholas' First Holy Communion took place shortly after they arrived back here and their family celebrated the event with us.

Jesus speaks to us through anyone he chooses

About four years later, we were at Angela's house for a Shabbat dinner on a Friday night. Nicholas was asking a lot of questions and making comparisons between their ritual and the Mass. After dinner, when Per and the children went into the living room, Angela asked me if I was still going to church. When I told her I was not, that I had issues with the Church, she told me that I should go to speak with the parish priest. If she had issues with her faith, she said, she would go to see the rabbi. I had known Angela for fourteen years and this was the first time she had ever criticised me like this and I was upset, but we dropped the conversation when we joined Per and the children in the living room.

The next morning, it was raining and Angela didn't go to the synagogue with Per and their daughter. Instead, she came for coffee and brought her very young son.

She told me that she knew she had offended me the night before. As I was waiting for an apology, she told me she was right to criticise me. We can't expect our children to turn out with the same values as we have, she said, unless we give them the benefit of the same kind of upbringing. She reminded me of the enormous sacrifices she had made to do that and she said she would not leave the house until I promised to go to talk to the parish priest. The best I was able to do was to promise I would think about it, but I didn't really have any intention of going to see him.

Meeting Jesus in the greengrocer's

As it happened, we needed something for lunch and, since it was raining, I ran down to the Broadway to pick it up. I said I would go to the shop, but I'd only go in if I found a parking spot right outside the greengrocer's – and I did – and, who should I find in the greengrocer's but Joe Cunningham, the parish priest! I laughed and I told him about Angela trying to persuade me to go to see him. His response: since God had gone to such lengths to create this coincidence, we should obviously meet.

I was blessed to have a parish priest that made the time to meet a number of times to talk, and eventually I was able to overcome the obstacle I had created and I agreed to go to Mass one Sunday morning.

"In England and Wales it's estimated that at least two-thirds of the baptised Catholic community is non-churchgoing"

Another chance encounter

At the end of that first Mass I went to, we saw two young black men cheerfully greeting people. At that time, our parish was almost entirely Irish and English and white. People went to Mass and afterwards they scurried away and, I thought, these two fellows obviously didn't know how to behave in this culture!

Nicholas went into the parish hall after Mass. When I went to get him, I saw that these two men had gone to the hall so I asked if he found out who they were. "They're Africans," he said, to which I replied, "I don't think I've ever met an African." "Oh, you will," he said, "I've invited them to come for dinner tonight."

The young men were seminarians of the Missionaries of Africa (also known as the White Fathers) and they were in London to study theology and they had been appointed to do pastoral work in our parish. We were going through a very difficult period. Nicholas was twelve years old; we had given up childcare after several bad experiences with au pairs after our long-term nanny had left.

We reached out to these two young foreigners and they reached out to us. We invited them to join in our activities and become part of our family. They were willing to come and spend time with Nicholas if

I was stuck in the office; they played tennis and chess with him – and they never accepted payment for the childminding they were doing.

The story of Philip and the Ethiopian eunuch is sometimes used when people are talking about working with people in my circumstances. We read in Acts 8:26-39 that an angel of the Lord said to Philip to get up and go down to Jerusalem. The Spirit told Philip to go over to the chariot going there, saying, "Go over to this chariot and join it." We are told that he "ran up to the chariot" and he found in it an Ethiopian eunuch reading the prophet Isaiah. Philip asked the eunuch if he understood what he was reading, to which he replied, "How can I unless someone guides me?"

Notice that Philip was asked to go to the Ethiopian eunuch; and he did. The eunuch told him he couldn't understand unless someone guided him. These two young missionaries searched me out after our initial meeting. They knew that I had just come back to the Church and I think they were curious to hear what questions I had, why I'd left and why I was coming back.

Nicholas and I both became close to Julian, who is a joyful, kind and wise man. When I was bad-tempered with Nicholas, he showed me by his example that there was a different way to respond to an issue with a child. When I was struggling with authority issues at work, he shared how he overcame similar issues. When I was approached by the parish priest a while after I had been regularly going to Mass and asked to read in the parish or to be a catechist, I felt I was not good enough to take on such roles.

Julian told me to read the first letter St Paul wrote to Timothy (1 Timothy 1:12-16). Paul writes that Christ judged him faithful and appointed him to his service even though he was formerly a blasphemer, a persecutor and a man of violence. Christ came into the world to save sinners. In this letter, Paul said he was the foremost of them and, for that very reason, he received mercy, so that in him Christ might display patience and make him an example to those who came to believe in him for eternal life.

I could identify with Paul. And I was willing to listen to what he had to say. With hindsight, I can see that the more I looked to Julian and the other White Fathers for guidance, the more my relationship with God was growing. I had begun to know Jesus.

Years later, Pope Francis described what had been happening to me in his first encyclical, *Evangelii Gaudium* ("The Joy of the Gospel"):

> The Gospel tells us to correct others and to help them to grow... without making judgments... our personal experience of being accompanied and assisted, and of openness to those who accompany us, will teach us to be patient and compassionate with others, and to find the right way to gain their trust, their openness and their readiness to grow. (EG 172)

When I look back, I find it humbling to think that God provided such a lot of personal and individual support and encouragement to me. I wonder if it was because he knew I was so stubborn that it was the only way to get through to me. Or, perhaps, he had things for me to do and, before I could do them, I needed to be thoroughly convinced (or should I say evangelised?).

Landings meetings

Some inactive Catholics who want to explore returning to the Church will find the welcome back they need through groups such as *Landings*, a Paulist programme for welcoming returning Catholics. It is a reconciliation process that helps faith communities welcome inactive Catholics who want to take another look at the Church. *Landings* trains compassionate lay people to reach out to those who have been away from the Church for any number of reasons.

The *Landings* meetings take place in a relaxed and friendly atmosphere where everyone gets a chance to share their faith journey. Participants often say what a relief it is to hear others had strayed from the Church for a time. They find it comforting not to be judged for their absence. Each participant is given a chance to explore why they had drifted away from the Church or how the Church had disillusioned them and why they have decided to return.

One returner said that she found that the Church atmosphere had changed from an authoritarian, judgemental presence to a much friendlier, accepting place where people share their faith. She also came to believe that **God loves us very much** – five of the most important words we ever hear.

Keeping in touch (KIT)

KIT is a lay ministry which through prayer, publicity and personal contact reaches out to, welcomes and keeps in touch with, all local Catholics, whether or not they go to church, with a special emphasis on home visiting.

Come Home For Christmas

Come Home For Christmas is an initiative of the Catholic Church which aims to offer a seasonal welcome to Catholics who for different reasons no longer or rarely attend Mass. They publicise locally and encourage parishioners to invite Catholics they know who are not practising.

Whatever a person's story or journey, the door's open. Whilst this resource has been created to offer a seasonal invitation and welcome, the journey back into the Catholic Community can of course happen at any time.

Chapter Seven: Reaching out to non-churchgoing Catholics

Crossing the threshold

In England and Wales it's estimated that at least two-thirds of the baptised Catholic community is non-churchgoing, which equates to approximately four to five million people. This makes for a significant constituency of people who, in most cases, self-identify as Catholic but never or rarely attend Mass.

The experience of staff at the Catholic Bishops' Conference of England and Wales (CBCEW), of diocesan personnel and of mission partners, is that parishes, and especially members who are parents and grandparents, repeatedly request information about resources and initiatives to help them reach out to this group of baptised non-churchgoing Catholics. They offer a practical guide on the process in order to respond to this area of pastoral and evangelistic need.

Points for reflection and discussion
- What does the Eucharist mean to you as an adult?
- How has your understanding of the Eucharist changed over the years and why?
- When we receive Communion, we are challenged to be like Christ in our thoughts and actions. How would you share that with a returning Catholic?

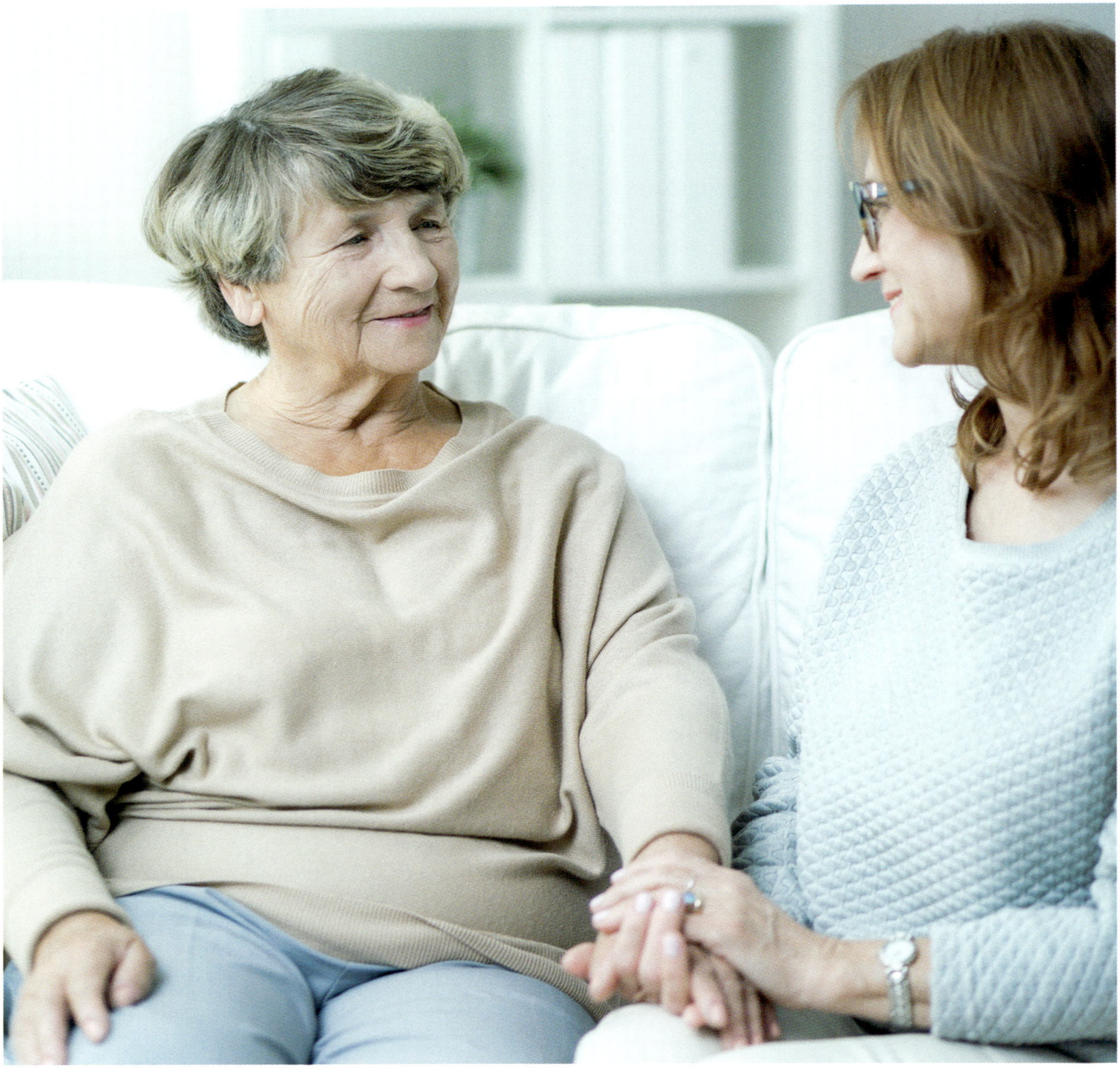

CHAPTER EIGHT

REACHING OUT TO THOSE WHO ARE SICK AND POOR

The role of the laity in the care of those who are sick and housebound is a parish ministry that has flourished in recent years. For example, extraordinary ministers of Holy Communion do not just take Holy Communion to them, but give generously of their time to help in many other ways. I have heard countless stories of people who attend to the material and social needs of those who are ailing.

Elderly neighbours are befriended and helped when they need it. Children of parents who are working often need childminding; sick neighbours are brought meals. Many parishes now offer bereavement counselling or (in the case of unqualified people) visiting.

Collecting food for the food bank has become a regular feature of many parishes. They are dealing with people who have been going hungry. These food banks have saved their lives and there are several instances of people where that's absolutely true; they had reached the end of their tether and they were planning to commit suicide. Food bank use in Britain is at record levels. More than one million food parcels, each providing enough food for three days, were given out between 2014 and 2015, more than 400,000 of which went to children.

Tom Grufferty says that the parish has become a "field hospital" – a place where we need to assure the sick, the elderly, the weak, the poor, the mentally ill, those suffering in any way, that we walk with them in their pain, but much more importantly, Jesus walks with them too.

Shekinah

In some parts of Africa the family unit joins forces with the hospital in providing food for the patient. While I was visiting Tamale in Ghana, I visited the Shekinah Clinic, established by the late Dr David Abdulai. He founded the Shekinah Clinic in 1989 as a philantropical medical facility that offers free medical services and accommodation to those who are destitute and homeless located in the Northern Region. He also established the annex at Wamale where he treated a great many hernia and HIV/Aids patients. And, he provided the poor and homeless with a daily food-on-wheels programme.

Shekinah is from the Hebrew verb which means "to settle, inhabit, or dwell" and that is why Dr David uses it as the name for his clinic. The word for the Tabernacle, *mishkan*, is a derivative of the same root as *Shekinah* and is used in the sense of dwelling-place in the Bible. For example, in Psalms 132:5 ("till I find a place for the LORD, a dwelling for the Mighty One of Jacob") and Numbers 24:5 ("How beautiful are your tents, Jacob, your dwelling places, Israel!" where the word for "your dwelling places" is *mishkenotecha*). Accordingly, in classic Jewish thought, the *Shekinah* refers to a dwelling or settling in a special sense, a dwelling or settling of divine presence. Without a doubt, I could feel the strong presence of God in that place.

The in-patient facility at Dr David's clinic consisted of a number of mud huts. Each patient was given a hut where she or he would stay with their family or carer(s) until they were ready to make the trip home. The day I was there, people were setting up a sound system so that the patients could listen to music. The families provided meals for their relatives while they were patients and they shared what they had with those who did not have food. I was very touched by this place and by Dr David, the most Christ-like person I have ever met, and I can easily see why the clinic was called Shekinah.

"The parish has become a 'field hospital' – a place where we need to assure the sick, the elderly, the weak, the poor, the mentally ill, those suffering in any way, that we walk with them in their pain"

Reaching out through appeals

I have a very special friend called Joan, a retired teacher who spent the first few years of her retirement in Kenya with the Mill Hill Missionaries, teaching their seminarians. Although she has been home for nearly twenty years, people she met in Kenya still write to her appealing for help with housing problems, medical bills, school fees, and so on, and she is very generous in her response to them. Not everyone has such personal contact with people who are lacking these most basic life needs.

Local appeals

Joan, like most of us, will do what she can when she comes face-to-face with people she meets who are in need and, like her, many of us are very generous by nature or by virtue of our Christian convictions. But, when we are unlikely to meet the people in need, there are many agencies who act on our behalf. Some of them are:

Foodbanks

Thirteen million people live below the poverty line in the UK, with individuals going hungry every day for a range of reasons, from benefit delays to receiving an unexpected bill on a low income. Foodbanks provide emergency food and support to people experiencing crisis in the UK. In 2015/16, we gave 1,109,309 three-day emergency food supplies to those people.

The Saint Vincent de Paul Society (SVP)

The vision of the SVP, which is inspired by Christ's message to love our neighbour as ourselves, is for individuals and families who are in any form of need to have hope together with a sense of dignity, worth, well-being and peace of mind. It is named after St Vincent de Paul, who said, "Let us serve the poor with a new kind of love." To serve the poor is to serve God.

Caritas

Caritas works with people on the margins of society: those in food poverty and debt, or suffering social isolation; those who are vulnerable: people with intellectual and physical disability; those who are homeless or at risk of exploitation.

The sick and retired priests' fund

This fund has helped hundreds of priests receive the care and support they need. Many priests working in England and Wales are due to retire from active ministry over the next twenty years and the Church needs our help to safeguard their future.

Priest training fund

This fund helps to support those who are being prepared for the priesthood and the Church needs our help to ensure their training.

Overseas missionary appeals

The staggering poverty of our brothers and sisters in other parts of the world can overwhelm us. We watch the news and the reality of the loss of life from warring factions – and the Western arms dealers who profit from it – in areas where there is famine. Food production and the ability to distribute it plummets. Through Aid to the Church in Need (ACN) we learn of violence and terrorism directed at Christians for practising their faith. We can also feel overwhelmed by reports of accidents or natural disasters. These tragedies can leave us feeling helpless. We can, however, reduce people's suffering and reduce disease and rates of mortality by donating what we can to the various Catholic agencies who can act on our behalf. They include:

Missio – overseas mission

The World Mission Sunday collection is sponsored by the Pontifical Mission Societies coordinated by Missio, the Catholic Church's official charity for overseas mission.

World Mission Sunday is our chance to show love and solidarity to our brothers and sisters overseas who share our faith. In offering our prayers, we join with missionaries everywhere in communion and compassion to support them in spreading the Good News, and by giving a donation we respond to Christ's call to feed the hungry and clothe the naked. Missio is responsible for coordinating World Mission Sunday and provides new, young or poor dioceses with the essential support they need on their journey to becoming self-sufficient. (*See*: <http://www.missio.org.uk/what-is-world-mission-sunday>, accessed 28 March 2017)

Missio raises awareness and fosters prayer and cooperation in the whole Church. With 120 offices worldwide, it is the only organisation which supports every one of the 1,069 mission dioceses around the world. The children's branch of Mission Together aims to teach children about the world through the true stories of children living overseas; they also emphasise the vital part that each child has to play in the mission of the Church and helping others.

Teaching children to be missionary

Pope Benedict XVI held a famous assembly during his visit to the United Kingdom in 2010 for 3,500 school children, and people were inspired by the way he engaged the children. No school would ever have that many children at one assembly; whatever the size of a school, it is always a challenge to find the most effective way of getting the children enthusiastically on board with a particular project.

Kasia Greenwood tells us about what the Mission Together team (the children's branch of Missio) do in "Engage the children" (*The Tablet*, 27 February 2016). This team have, for a number of years, been providing assemblies and other resources free of charge to primary schools, through a network of experienced volunteers and downloadable materials.

Kasia told us about one volunteer, who was promoting the famous "Red Box" – which is used to collect coins to aid the work of Missio (with APF-Mill Hill) and Mission Together. The volunteer brought out a slightly larger demonstration copy of the box and placed a coin into it. Not unlike the magic trick of pulling a rabbit out of a hat, she then proceeded to open the box to reveal what this donation had "turned into" in terms of the work it enables missionaries to do for children all over the world.

A rosary symbolised how the money would be used to support catechesis and spirituality; a plaster represented the important work the missionaries do to offer children healthcare; a small pencil represented how the money would be used for education; a toy house symbolised how it would help to shelter children; and a satsuma signified food they would be able to give the children.

Encouraging the children to participate actively and to make a connection between the message and life experience helps the participants to remember the message being communicated. This use of a visual learning tool had a great impact in capturing the imagination of the young audience as well as getting the message across that the pounds and pennies that are put into these boxes go to fund the vital work of the Catholic Church abroad by bringing God's love and hope to the poorest and most in need.

Kasia said that the message behind a Mission Together assembly is that we are all called to be missionaries – children as well as adults. Being a missionary need not always mean leaving behind your home and family in order to travel overseas to live and work with the poor, as some adults do. Sharing God's love with others by using our talents and making a commitment to make small sacrifices and pray for those in need is something we can all do. Missionary children have something so special to offer – their own particular understanding and compassion for children in the rest of the world – thus the Mission Together motto: "children helping children".

CAFOD

CAFOD (Catholic Agency for Overseas Development) is an international development charity and the official aid agency of the Catholic Church in England and Wales. It stands beside people living in poverty – whatever their religion or culture. Through local church partners, we help people directly in their own communities, and campaign for global justice.

Guided by the values of compassion, solidarity and hope, it is rooted in the Catholic community. Together, with the help of volunteers, CAFOD puts our faith into action to help our sisters and brothers living in extreme poverty to reach their full potential, regardless of religion or culture. CAFOD is a member of Caritas International – a group of over 160 Catholic agencies from around the world – known as "the helping hand of the Church". Because CAFOD works through the local Church, they can reach people and places that others can't.

Home Mission

Each year on Home Mission Sunday, the bishops invite parishes to pray for our home mission – the domestic Church, outreach, evangelisation and new evangelisation. On this day, the bishops invite parishes to pray for home mission.

Home Mission Sunday supports the work of evangelisation in England and Wales. On this day we are encouraged to pray for the work of evangelisation in England and Wales, remembering in our prayers especially those whom we know are distant from the life of faith.

The Bishops' Conference of England and Wales launched a document on crime and punishment in 2004 called "A Place of Redemption". It approaches complex questions – the rights of society and the victims of crime as well as the rights of prisoners and models of rehabilitation. Above all, it insists that the dignity and value of the human person should never be lost or erased.

As a result, an intensive resettlement project called Basic Caring Communities (BACC) was established to provide support from groups of faith-motivated volunteers to build social networks and provide emotional and practical support. The service provides support in prison and continues for three months on release, providing contact on a daily basis by phone, one-to-one and through group support.

In addition, the Prison Advice and Care Trust (Pact) is a national charity that provides support to prisoners, people with convictions and their families. They support people to make a fresh start, and minimise the harm that can be caused by imprisonment to people who have committed offences, to families and to communities.

Many prison inmates find their sentence is a time for a deeply personal soul-searching. As a result, some people discover God and, hidden from public gaze, try to turn their lives around. In 2016 Redemptorist Publications published *Faith Inside – a guide for Catholics in prison*. It is the first-ever catechetical resource uniquely tailored to the needs of Catholics in UK prisons. There is now an *Alpha for Prisons* and various RCIA resources that can be used with those prisoners who want to deepen their faith or to become Catholic.

Points for reflection and discussion

Take a little time to look at Kurt Welther's painting of St Vincent de Paul on the opposite page and read the description that accompanies it, below.

- Do we see the face of Jesus Christ in the poor and downtrodden, in those who are oppressed, have no voice, are despised?
- Is St Vincent de Paul an inspiration for us in a world that is cynical about the goodness of God?

Vincent de Paul is sitting among the poor in this picture as one of them. He has no halo, he does not stand above them as the great helper. But who are the poor? Sitting here are old people and between them children with deep-set eyes. We can see a tattooed man just released from prison, a vagabond and people from foreign countries, refugees. Their faces are not very clear. Vincent says: "Often enough the poor have no faces at all, but if you flip over the coin, you will see, in the light of faith, that the Son of God is coming to us here through the poor." It is as if all the people had just come in as Vincent was about to sit down and eat his simple meal. Now he is sharing it with them. The face of Christ that shines from the centre of the table gives us an idea of the presence of Christ in these people.

(Based on a meditation by Fr Pulcher, adapted by the author)

Chapter Eight: Reaching out to those who are sick and poor

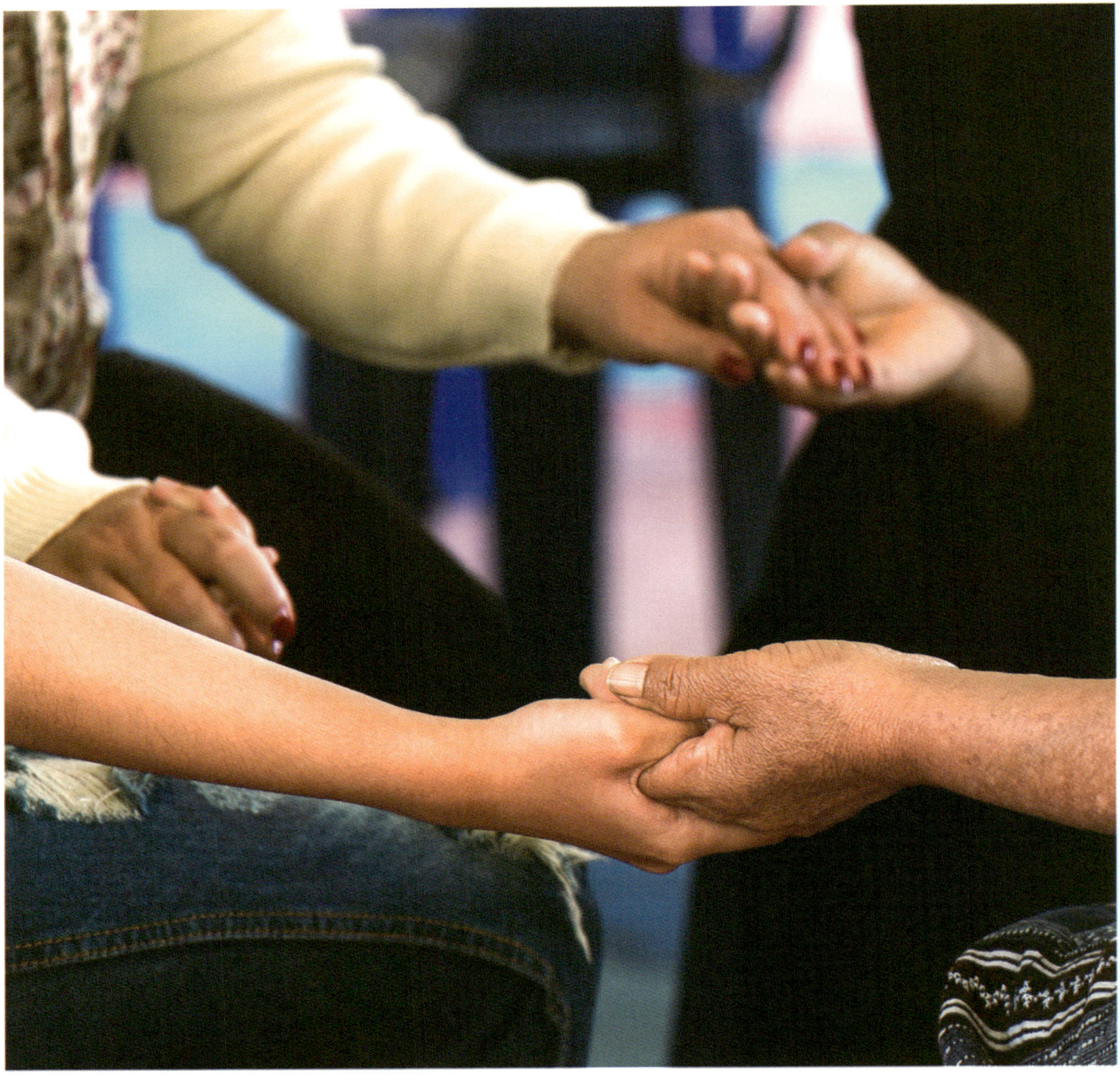

CHAPTER NINE

WHEN TWO OR THREE ARE GATHERED IN MY NAME, I AM THERE

In Matthew 18:20 we read Jesus' beautiful words to us, "When two or three of you are gathered in my name, I am there." These words are a reminder that we need to gather even in the smallest groups to honour the Lord and to let his saving power transform us and the world.

More and more people are convinced that basic parish communities are at the heart of parish renewal, where parishioners are enabled to reflect in a personal way on the word of God, on their faith and on their call to holiness and discipleship of Jesus in their daily lives.

As we entered the third millennium, there was an urgent call from St John Paul II to every diocese to engage in renewal and evangelisation. The document, *Novo Millennio Ineunte* ("At the Beginning of a New Millennium") meditates on the story in Luke's Gospel when Jesus urges the disciples/fishermen – although they had caught nothing all night – to "launch out into the deep" (Luke 5:4). It is worth reading the passage from Luke 5:1-5 (*NRSV*):

Once while Jesus was standing beside the lake of Gennesaret, and the crowd was pressing in on him to hear the word of God, he saw two boats there at the shore of the lake; the fishermen had gone out of them and were washing their nets. He got into one of the boats, the one belonging to Simon, and asked him to put out a little way from the shore. Then he sat down and taught the crowds from the boat. When he had finished speaking, he said to Simon, "Put out into the deep water and let down your nets for a catch." Simon answered, "Master, we have worked all night long but have caught nothing. Yet if you say so, I will let down the nets."

At Your Word, Lord

Cardinal Cormac Murphy-O'Connor offered the diocese in Westminster the same challenge in 2003. The diocese responded using a form of the words St Peter spoke to Jesus, "At your word, Lord" (Luke 5:5). At Your Word, Lord (AYWL) became the name for the pastoral and spiritual renewal programme that, in my opinion, changed the face of the diocese. Speaking for myself and my experience of being part of the programme in my parish, I could see first-hand the transformation that took place in people.

The origin of the idea for AYWL

Yves Congar in a book called *Lay People in the Church* was the inspiration. In it, he speaks about small communities, which he calls "cells". Cardinal Cormac says he remembers reading it and thinking: he's right. Then he wrote an article for the *Clergy Review* about small communities. That was well before he became a bishop. He started forming and encouraging small communities in Arundel and Brighton where he was first a bishop. The launch of At Your Word, Lord at Wembley Arena attracted 20,000 people.

In his foreword to the book *Small Christian Communities Today*, the Cardinal says renewal in the Church always comes about through small cells of men and women. St Francis had his companions. So did St Dominic and St Teresa. Cardinal Cormac says that he started these small groups as a curate in Portsmouth and he saw the effect it had on those who took part. He explains in the foreword that, towards the end of his period in his first parish, a group of people invited him to join their monthly meetings. They met in different houses to pray, to read a passage of the Gospel, and to reflect on the circumstances of their daily lives. This, he says, was his first lesson in the value of a "Basic Christian Community".

In his next parish, he helped to form ten of these basic communities. Before long, out of a parish of a thousand or so practising Catholics, about two hundred people were meeting regularly. It was in these faith clusters, or communities, that a whole mix of people – married, unmarried, young and old – discovered a new and deeper experience of faith through prayer, scripture, community and service to others. It was through these small communities, the Cardinal says, that the parish came alive.

Perhaps today, he reflects, we are coming to understand with greater clarity that all baptised Christians are called to the responsibility of evangelisation. It begins with each person accepting the word of God. In accepting that word more fully, individually, and as a community, we become more committed to Christ and to his will for us in our lives.

These are the reasons that basic parish communities were at the heart of the programme for parish renewal in At Your Word, Lord, which he initiated in the Diocese of Westminster. The Cardinal says you can't be a Catholic today unless you belong to some kind of group, some kind of cell. You could say the cell is family, then is extended through the parish and the diocese. But, beyond that, the cell is fellow Catholics you meet with, read the Gospel with.

Basic Christian Communities

These small communities are also known as Basic Christian Communities, Basic Ecclesial Communities, Base Ecclesial Communities or Ecclesial Basic

Communities. The communities are considered as a new way of "being the Church" – the Church at the grassroots, in neighbourhoods and villages. The earliest communities emerged in Brazil and in the Philippines in the late 1960s and later spread to Africa, Asia and in recent times to Australia and North America.

The ordinary faithful are enabled to exercise the common priesthood by actively participating in the liturgical celebrations. They participate in Christ's kingly mission by their loving service to others, especially those who are poor and in need, their work for justice and peace, for social transformation. Thus, in many parts of the world, BCCs are referred to as prophetic (evangelising), priestly (worshipping) and kingly (serving) communities echoing Vatican II's vision of the Church as the People of God.

In his encyclical *Redemptoris Missio*, Pope St John Paul II affirmed that,

> [BCCs are] centres for Christian formation and missionary outreach... [They] are a sign of vitality within the Church, an instrument of formation and evangelization, a solid starting point for a new society based on a "civilisation of love." [BCCs] decentralise and organise the parish community, to which they always remain united. They take root in less privileged and rural areas, and become a leaven of Christian life, of care for the poor, and of commitment to the transformation of society... [They are] a means of evangelisation and of initial proclamation of the Gospel, and a source of new ministries... And the Synod of Bishops, stated, "Because the Church is communion, the new 'basic communities', if they truly live in unity with the Church, are a true expression of communion and a means for the construction of a more profound communion. They are a cause for great hope for the life of the Church." (RM 51)

Alpha works for the same reasons

Fr James Mallon is a parish priest in a remote part of Canada. He has turned his parish into a powerhouse for evangelisation by introducing basic parish communities.

I interviewed James a couple of years ago and he told me that, at thirty-one years of age, when he was pastoring his first parish, he sequestered the parish hall on Monday nights for the ten-week programme of evangelisation called the Alpha Course. The hall was booked for a card-playing group who were not happy to change their booking. One woman shouted at him, "We don't need to know about Jesus. We need to play cards!" He said that "the uproar was so great that an emergency meeting of the parish council had to be called." In spite of advice from others to back off, he says he stubbornly pushed ahead. He has been a big supporter of Alpha since then. He simply says, "It works."

"We don't need to know about Jesus. We need to play cards!"

I asked James what the secret of Alpha is. He explained that it embraces the **belong-believe-behave** approach to evangelisation. It creates a warm, welcoming, nonthreatening, non-pressurised and non-judgemental environment. They use the standard Alpha course: a series of interactive sessions to discuss the Christian faith in an informal, fun and friendly environment. It looks at topics such as "Who is Jesus?" and "Why and how do I pray?" and there is an option of a weekend away.

All over the world, Alpha groups follow this same process. They meet for a meal, and then there is a talk followed by discussion in small groups. Through the ten-week process, James told me "trust begins to build as meals are shared and participants are listened to in small groups" – and, as people begin to let their guard down, they get the message. James said, "The truth of Jesus and his Gospel begins to knock on the door of their hearts and, by the end of the ten weeks, many of them have been led to a personal encounter with Jesus and make the decision to follow him." And, as they experience this encounter, he sees their "lives changed and transformed; they come alive in their experience of God's family, the Church."

James told me that he thinks that Alpha is the most effective tool he has found to date; it is at the centre of his parish's evangelistic efforts. When I spoke to him, they had recently concluded eight different Alpha courses running concurrently, with over 350 guests, about a third of whom were non-churchgoers. He said that the parish "hosts daytime Alphas, Friday night Alphas, Thursday night Alphas, Pub Alpha, Sushi Alpha (where they take over an entire sushi restaurant), Youth Alpha in the parish and in the local state school, Alpha in a community centre, Alpha by the Hearth (in homes) and Alpha in prison." All these courses are run by the parishioners, many of whom have experienced conversion and transformation through their own experience of Alpha – and, through their involvement with these groups, they grow and deepen in their relationship with Christ thereby keeping the momentum going.

More and more people are convinced that these basic parish communities are at the heart of parish renewal, where parishioners are enabled to reflect in a personal way on the word of God, on their faith and on their call to holiness and discipleship of Jesus in their daily lives. In addition, those who have completed Alpha are offered a wide assortment of catechetical programmes so that they can continue their formation and journey towards maturity.

Points for reflection and discussion

- What is your experience of small Christian groups?
- Did you become more committed to Christ and to his will for us in our lives through a small Christian group?
- What single event comes to your mind when you ask yourself the question, "When did I make a conscious choice to know and follow Jesus?"

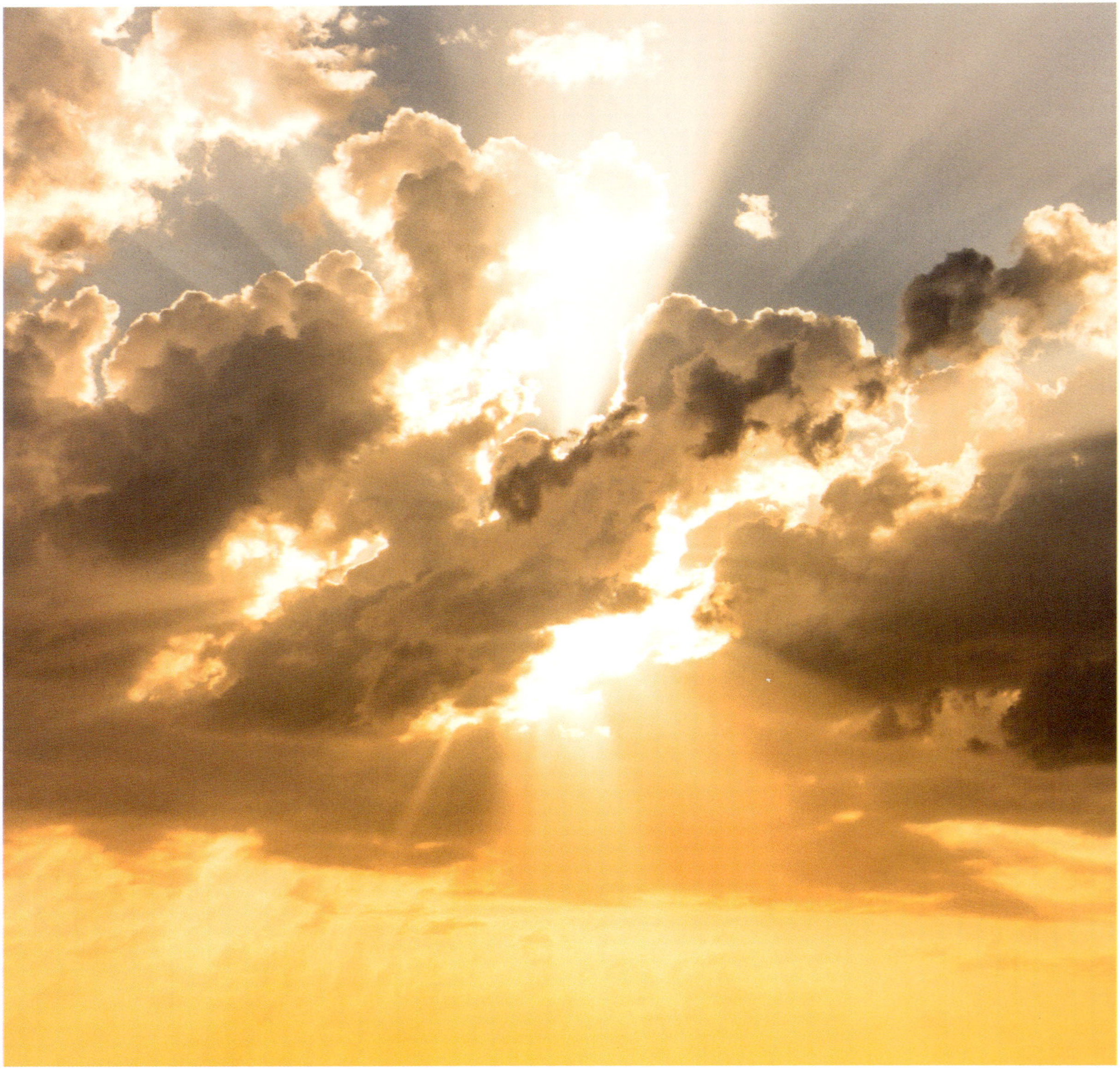

CHAPTER TEN

GO TELL EVERYONE THE NEWS THAT THE KINGDOM OF GOD HAS COME

I began this book with a definition of evangelisation I found on a leaflet produced by the Home Mission Desk of the Bishops' Conference of England and Wales:

> Evangelisation is the sharing of the Good News of Jesus and the starting point is our relationship with him. It's about proclaiming our faith in him, by living it out in service and witness.

The main body of the book comprised stories of the various times and ways in which we encounter Christ through others or others encounter Christ in us in service and witness. My hope was and is that the stories will spark memories of the times when we have made a conscious choice to know and follow Jesus and that these memories will reaffirm our desire to draw others to Christ.

The Christian Gospel is the Good News of Jesus Christ, the fulfilment of the promised kingdom. To evangelise is to make known the Good News of Jesus Christ and it is about sharing our personal experience of it. I hope that you have been convinced by what you have read on the pages of this book to agree that the encounters I describe are rich in potential for all of us. However, if we lack awareness and sensitivity to the possibilities inherent within them, we can easily miss or overlook the opportunities of evangelisation in these encounters.

It is Jesus we encounter in serving others and it is his love, the grace he gives us in his teachings and the sacraments, that should inspire our encounters, our evangelisation, for he does indeed have the message of joy, the liberating message of love and of eternal life.

REFERENCES AND RESOURCES

Church documents referred to in the text

Ad Gentes ("To the Nations", Decree on the Mission Activity of the Church), Second Vatican Council, 7 December 1965.

Amoris Laetitia ("The Joy of Love"), Pope Francis, 18 April 2016.

Catechesi Tradendae ("On Catechesis in Our Time", to the Episcopate, the Clergy and the Faithful of the Entire Catholic Church), Pope John Paul II, 16 October 1979.

Dei Verbum ("Word of God", Decree on Divine Revelation), Second Vatican Council, 18 November 1965.

Evangelii Gaudium ("The Joy of the Gospel"), Pope Francis, 24 November 2013.

Evangelii Nuntiandi ("Proclaiming the Gospel", Evangelisation in the Modern World), Pope Paul VI, 8 December 1975.

Guidelines for the Preparation of Couples for Marriage, Department for Christian Responsibility and Citizenship, Catholic Bishops' Conference of England and Wales (London: Rejoice Publications, 2016).

Instruction on certain questions regarding the collaboration of the non-ordained faithful in the sacred ministry of the priest, Congregation of the Clergy, et al., 15 August 1997.

Novo Millennio Ineunte ("At the Beginning of the New Millennium"), Pope John Paul II, 1 June 2001.

One Bread One Body: a teaching document on the Eucharist in the lift of the Church, Catholic Bishops' Conference of England and Wales, 1998.

Redemptoris Missio ("Mission of the Redeemer", On the Permanent Validity of the Church's Missionary Mandate), Pope John Paul II, 7 December 1990.

Rite of Christian Initiation of Adults, Office of the Sacred Congregation for Divine Worship, (including Part II: *Christian Initiation of Children of Catechetical Age*), 19 February 1987.

Sacrosanctum Concilium ("Sacred Council", Constitution on the Sacred Liturgy), Second Vatican Council, 4 December 1963.

Valuing Difference: People with disabilities in the life and mission of the Church, Bishops' Conference of England and Wales, 1998.

Books referred to in the text

John Arnold, *The Quality of Mercy: A Fresh Look at the Sacrament of Reconciliation* (London: St Pauls Publishing, 1993).

Steven Bevans SVD, *Models of Contextual Theology* (Maryknoll, New York: Orbis Books, 1997).

Yves Congar OP, *Lay People in the Church* (Westminster, Maryland: Newman Press, 1965).

Erik Erikson, *Identity and the Life Cycle* (New York, New York: Norton, 1980).

Thomas Groome, *Educating for Life – A Spiritual Vision for Every Teacher and Parent*, (Allen, Texas: Thomas More Publishers, 1998).

—— *Christian Religious Education – Sharing Our Story and Vision* (New York, New York: Harper Collins Publishers, 1980).

Gerard W. Hughes SJ, *Oh God, Why?* (Oxford: The Bible Reading Fellowship, 1993).

James Mallon, *Divine Renovation: From a Maintenance to a Missionary Parish* (New London, Connecticut: Twenty-Third Publications, 2014).

Denis McBride C.Ss.R., *Emmaus: the Gracious Visit of God according to Luke* (Dublin: Dominican Publications, 1991).

Eddie McGhee, *Faith Inside: a guide for Catholics in prison* (Chawton: Redemptorist Publications, 2016).

Joseph G. Healy and Jeanne Hinton, eds, *Small Christian Communities Today*, with a foreword by Cormac Murphy-O'Connor (Maryknoll, New York: Orbis Books, 2005).

Daniel O'Leary, *Already Within* (Dublin: Columba Press, 2007).

Edward Schillebeeckx OP, *Christ the Sacrament of Encounter with God* (London: Sheed and Edward Ward, 1966).

Sherry Waddell, *Forming Intentional Disciples* (Huntington, Indiana: Our Sunday Visitor, 2012).

Articles referred to in the text

Catholic News Service, "Encounter God's mercy in Confession" 23 August 2016.

Bernard Cotter, "Another kind of send-off", Parish Practice, *The Tablet*, 9 November 2013.

Kasia Greenwood, "Engage the children", Schools Practice, *The Tablet*, 27 February 2016.

Tom Grufferty, "Street credibility", Parish Practice, *The Tablet*, 19 March 2016.

Sheila Keefe, "How welcoming are our parishes?" *The Pastoral Review*, March-April 2007.

Maureen Knight, "Scotland preparing for lay led funerals", *Catholic Truth* (quoting *Scottish Catholic Observer* as source), 16 November 2016.

Ulick Loring, "Home truths", Parish Practice, *The Tablet*, 12 May 2012.

Liz O'Brien and Diana Klein, "One bread, one body", Parish Practice, *The Tablet*, 28 January 2012.

Jane Shields, "A place for all", Parish Practice, *The Tablet*, 21 June 2008.

Tablet Editorial, "What the Church can learn from the young", *The Tablet*, 19 January 2017.

Reference

Catechism of the Catholic Church, 2nd ed. (Vatican: Libreria Editrice Vaticana, 2000).

Code of Canon Law (London: Collins Liturgical Publications, 1983).

General Directory of Catechesis (London: Catholic Truth Society, 1997).

I Call You Friends: Living and Sharing Our Faith: A National Project of Catechesis and Religious Education of the Catholic Bishops' Conference of England and Wales (Great Wakering: McCrimmons, 2010).

Web references and resources

ACN (Aid to the Church in Need)
<http://www.acnuk.org>

Alpha in a Catholic context
<http://alpha.org/catholic-context/home>

CAFOD (Catholic Agency For Overseas Development)
<https://www.cafod.org.uk>

Caritas
<http://www.caritas.org>

Come Home For Christmas (a seasonal resource)
<http://www.comehomeforchristmas.co.uk>

Crossing the Threshold
<http://www.cbcew.org.uk/CBCEW-Home/Departments/Evangelisation-and-Catechesis/Crossing-the-Threshold-Non-Churchgoing-Catholics/Crossing-the-Threshold-Resources-eManual/Introduction>

Disability awareness
John McCorkell, Founder and Director of It's All Normal promotes and teaches the inclusion of disabled people. John can be contacted through his website or through social media.

<http://www.itsallnormal.com>

Everybody's Welcome
The Everybody's Welcome website can be found on the website of the Bishops' Conference of England and Wales:

<http://www.cbcew.org.uk/CBCEW-Home/Departments/Christian-Responsibility-and-Citizenship/Marriage-and-Family-Life/Everybody-s-Welcome>

Some of the Everybody's Welcome top tips for busy parishes can be found on:

<http://www.catholicfamily.org.uk/wp-content/uploads/2014/02/TopTipsforBusyParishes.pdf>

Growing Up Catholic
<http://www.growingupcatholic.com>

Home Mission Sunday
<http://www.catholicnews.org.uk>

KIT (Keeping in touch)
<http://www.kit4catholics.org.uk>

Landings (UK):
<https://landings.org.uk>

Marriage and Family Life
<http://www.catholicfamily.org.uk/what-we-do/marriage/marriage-preparation/guidelines-for-marriage-preparation>

Missio
<http://www.missio.org.uk>

Pact (Prison Advice and Care Trust) [H4]
<https://www.prisonadvice.org.uk>

Pope Francis: Angelus address inspires Birmingham Diocese help to homeless, 9 January 2017
<http://www.birminghamdiocese.org.uk/2017/01/archbishop-helps-birmingham-city-centre-soup-kitchen>

Pope Francis explains: On how to be a good confessor
<https://zenit.org/articles/popes-tips-on-how-to-be-a-good-confessor>

Pope Francis' World Mission Day 2017 address: "Mission at the heart of the Christian faith", 4 June 2017
<http://w2.vatican.va/content/francesco/en/messages/missions/documents/papa-francesco_20170604_giornata-missionaria2017.html>

SVP (St Vincent de Paul Society)
<https://svp.org.uk>

Welcoming older people
Growing Old Grace-*fully*
<http://www.growingoldgracefully.org.uk>
For the guide, *Welcoming Older People: ideas for and from parishes*, go to <http://www.growingoldgracefully.org.uk> (click on the tab marked "Resources")

(Web references last accessed 5 June 2017.)

Special acknowledgements

I am very grateful to Bernard Cotter and to Aidan Galvin CM for reading my drafts and for their encouragement.